Carving Twigs and Branches

Carving Twigs and Branches

Ernest C. Lubkemann, Jr.

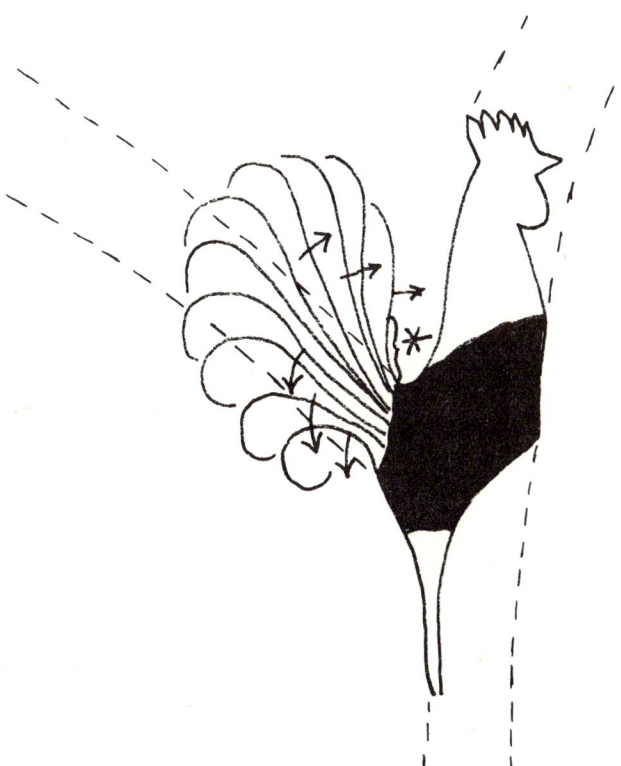

 Sterling Publishing Co., Inc. New York

Photographs by Jim Moore and Ernest C. Lubkemann, Jr.

Library of Congress Cataloging in Publication Data

Lubkemann, Ernest C.
   Carving twigs and branches.
   (Home craftsman series)
   Includes index.
   1. Wood-carving. I. Title. II. Series.
TT199.7.L82   736'.4   81-50980
ISBN 0-8069-7532-6 (pbk.)   AACR2

Second Printing, 1982

Copyright © 1981 by Ernest C. Lubkemann, Jr.
Published by Sterling Publishing Co., Inc.
Two Park Avenue, New York, N.Y. 10016
Distributed in Australia by Oak Tree Press Co., Ltd.
P.O. Box K514 Haymarket, Sydney 2000, N.S.W.
Distributed in the United Kingdom by Blandford Press
Link House, West Street, Poole, Dorset BH15 1LL, England
Distributed in Canada by Oak Tree Press Ltd.
℅ Canadian Manda Group, 215 Lakeshore Boulevard East
Toronto, Ontario M5A 3W9
Manufactured in the United States of America
All rights reserved
Library of Congress Catalog Card No.: 81-8764
Sterling ISBN 0-8069-7532-6 Paper

CONTENTS

Preface 7

Introduction 9

Supplies 11

All About Wood 15

Cutting 23

The Rooster 27

Other Projects 55

Index 96

To My Family
Sheri, Steve, Sharon, and David,
Dad, Mom, Judy,
Bill, Frieda, Jon, Andy, and Sarah,
and Mom Hall

And to Dr. John W. Luke,
who first showed me how a rooster
could emerge from a little twig

PREFACE

In this age of the ready-made and store-bought, many of us are missing out on the pleasure of accomplishment and plain old fun and relaxation. What I want to share with you in this book is unique. I hope it will open up for you a whole new world of imaginative creativity and provide a lot of good fun in the process—and even some works of art! All at very little expense!

Certainly the idea of whittling a rooster or pheasant from a tree fork isn't original with me. I remember seeing a wood-fork rooster for the first time in the western North Carolina mountains some years ago. Though the style of those Carolina roosters is quite different from what you will be seeing in the following pages, the basic idea is the same. Where the craft actually started, I don't know, but I suspect it was somewhere in Europe. Some time after I began whittling roosters I saw one that was vaguely similar that had been imported from Scandinavia, as I remember. More recently someone told me that a couple of her uncles in Europe also made roosters from branches.

The enthusiasm for this hobby has been very encouraging, both in the United States and Canada, as well as in Europe—especially Portugal, where the rooster is practically a national symbol. It has been a satisfying experience to see people of all ages learn what they can do with a few little branches.

One wonderfully encouraging fact: You don't have to be a natural-born woodcarver to work with twigs and branches. In fact, people who have tried their hand at regular wood carving and haven't been too successful will probably be very surprised at how much easier they find carving with twigs and branches.

I'm grateful to the folks in the Blue Ridge Mountains of North Carolina for the idea that they shared with me. Many other people have offered encouragement along the way, and I want to thank them for their interest and help. A special thank you to Dr. John W. Luke and the whittlers of the Carolina mountains for contributing the idea; thanks also go to Mr. Daniel Gluck and Mr. John F. Thomas III as well, for all the enthusiasm they

Preface

have shown and the encouragement they have given. Thank you to all the people at Sterling Publishing Company, for their advice, encouragement and hard work; all the people in North America and Europe, who have demonstrated how easy it is to learn this technique; the members of my family, who have always been enthusiastic supporters; and to the thousands of individuals in so many places who have simply enjoyed these little wooden creations.

As far as the book itself goes, I've tried to make it fun to read and follow. This isn't always easy to do, especially in a publication that must at times drift into sounding like a manual. Nevertheless, I think you'll enjoy your experience and come up with a lot of projects that you're pleased with.

Have Fun!
E. C. L., Jr.

1

INTRODUCTION

If you use your imagination, there's no telling what you might think of carving from a twig or branch. With a little practice, you can readily make the projects shown in the following pages. Every carving that you make will be an original, different in at least some small way from every other one that you or anyone else has made.

This particular approach to woodworking uses branches of all shapes and sizes—branches that are blown down by the wind, branches from the woods, and branches from your own backyard. It does not require expensive or hard-to-get materials.

The main project here is the rooster. Roosters are popular for home decoration, but the basic reason for using them is that they demonstrate so easily the effects possible with a knife and a twig or branch. To be sure, a rooster isn't the only thing you can make from a wood fork, but the techniques used are the same ones used to whittle almost anything else. Once you know how to carve a rooster, you can try your hand at many other figures.

Fig. 1.

Carving Twigs and Branches

Fig. 2. Most projects in this book call for twigs and branches that are less than 1½" (3.8 cm) in diameter.

Fig. 3.

2

SUPPLIES

The most important tools needed to carve from twigs and branches are a couple of very sharp knife blades. A good-quality pocketknife works beautifully, provided it is well sharpened. Alternatively, X-Acto knives are readily available, are very sharp, and come in a variety of useful shapes and sizes. Blades #0101, #0105, #24, #26, and #27, which fit into the #2, #5, and #6 handles, will enable you to work on any of the projects in this book.

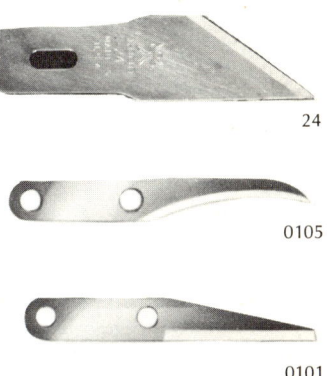

24

0105

0101

Fig. 4.

26

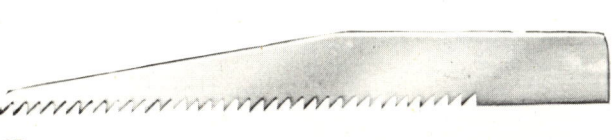

27

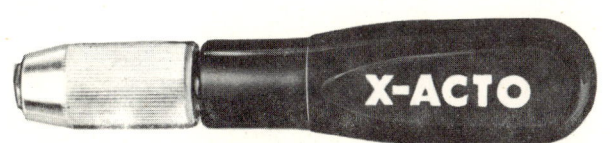

Carving Twigs and Branches

The other equipment you will need depends upon how you decide to finish your projects. The items you will probably want are:

>   white glue
>   a medium-sized nail
>   fine-grade sandpaper
>   enamel paint, red, yellow, black
>   2–3 good-quality paintbrushes, including sizes 0 or 1 and 2 or 3
>   paint thinner, for cleaning brushes
>   shellac or polyurethane, for finishing figures
>   sharpening stone

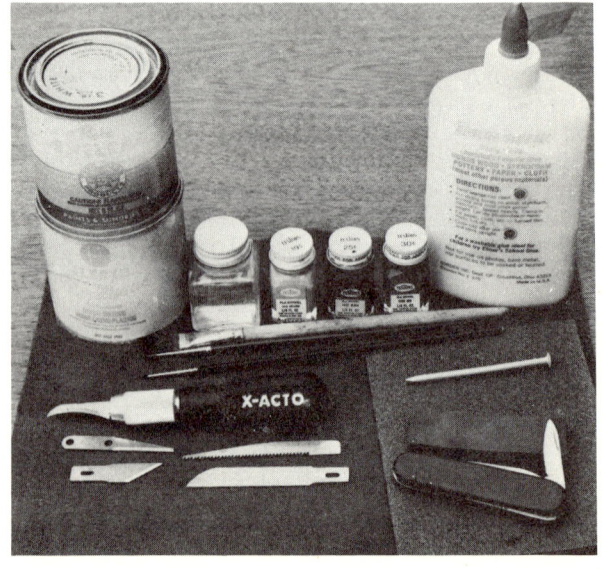

Fig. 5. You may prefer to leave your projects unfinished, especially if you use non-glossy paints.

Supplies

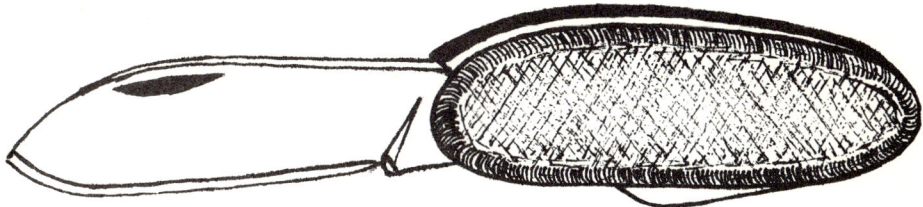

Figs. 6a. & 6b. Sharpen both sides of your new blade to remove the tiny ridges, and to smooth the sides.

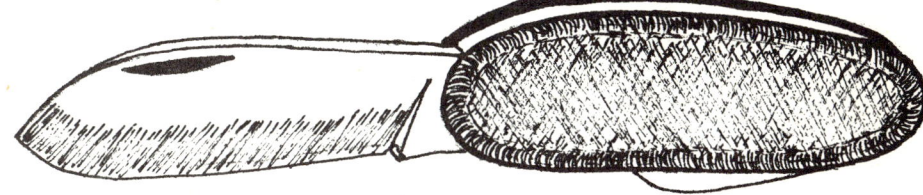

A good pocketknife for the projects in this book should have one large blade and one small one. Use the large blade for the rough cutting and for making curls in the wood—to make things like the rooster's tail feathers. Use the small blade to get into close spots. Both blades must be very sharp. The factory edge of a newly purchased knife may feel sharp, but don't let it fool you. A proper edge for fine work should look like fig. 6b. To get this result, sharpen your knife by holding it nearly flat against the sharpening stone. Don't be afraid to scratch the polished finish on the side of the blade. Use a circular motion at first, and a straight motion only for the final strokes across the stone.

Carving Twigs and Branches

Fig. 7. If you were to take a cross-section of the knife blade before and after filing away the ridge and smoothing the sides, this is what you'd see.

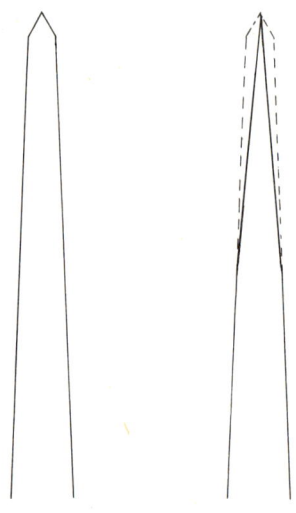

Figs. 8a. & 8b. To get the smaller blade into shape for whittling, you will have to file it down slightly.

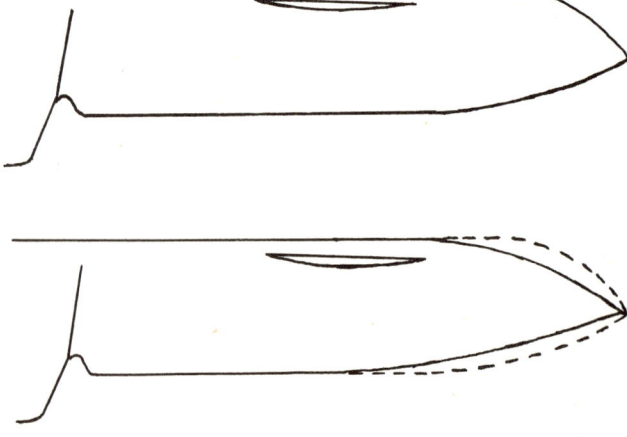

3

ALL ABOUT WOOD

Most of the projects in this book call for small twigs and branches less than 1½″ (38 mm) in diameter. If you want to test your concentration, you can use little twigs as thin as 1/32″ (0.80 mm) for some truly miniature work!

Carving with branches and twigs doesn't necessarily require a softwood such as white pine. Harder woods are often better to work with. Whether the wood should be absolutely fresh, bone-dry, hard, or soft, depends on the object you're making. For some projects, it really doesn't matter whether the wood was cut that day or years before. However, it is better to avoid old wood that is beginning to deteriorate. If a twig or branch is so brittle that it snaps cleanly in two pieces when you bend it, it's probably too dry.

Fig. 9. Ball-point pen. Chances are the hole you drill won't be long enough to hold a full-length refill, so you'll have to cut the refill down to the proper length.

Carving Twigs and Branches

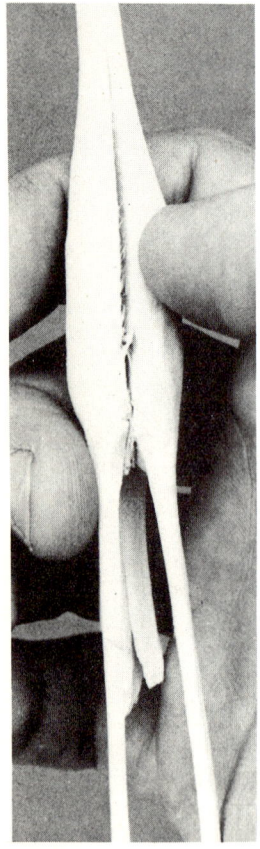

Fig. 10. You can imagine, I wasn't all that thrilled when this newly carved heron quickly developed a wide split. It's better to let fresh wood dry for two or three days before whittling.

If you cut a live branch, you may need to let the wood dry for a few days before beginning to work with it, because some very fresh wood tends to split as it dries. Green wood also does not produce the nice curls that drier wood does.

For most of the projects described, you'll need only relatively small branches and twigs. Often you'll find just what you need right in your own neighborhood. Failing that, you can get started by doing the "no-branch" projects with a piece of doweling or even an old broom handle.

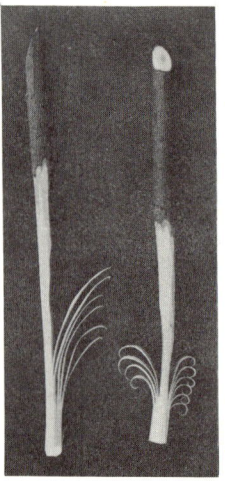

Fig. 11. The freshly cut stick on the left will not produce the curls that the drier (though not completely dry) one on the right will.

All About Wood

SELECTING WOOD

No matter what type of wood you have in your area, there are four basic guidelines for choosing the best branches to work with when you're making a rooster.

1. *The pith (the soft, spongy section in the very center of the branch) should be small.* A branch ½" (12.70 mm) in diameter should have a pith no thicker than 1/16" (1.6 mm). A thick pith may force you to make the rooster's comb too fat!

Fig. 12. This is the size of the pith for a branch of this width.

2. *The wood should be relatively firm and hard.* When a hardwood branch is still fairly fresh, it's quite easy to work with. Even when wood such as oak or swamp maple is completely dry, working with the smaller twigs is not too difficult.

3. *There should be no sticky sap.*

4. *There should be no knots or other branches around the fork.* This rule applies mainly to projects like birds. As your skills develop, you'll begin to see difficulties such as inconveniently located knots as challenges.

17

Carving Twigs and Branches

KINDS OF WOOD

Several kinds of wood are good for the projects in this book. If you can't obtain any of these woods, keep in mind the basic guidelines and you'll be able to find something else perfectly acceptable.

Swamp maple (which doesn't grow only in swamps) is one of the very best woods to work with. Many of the samples pictured in this book are made of swamp maple. *Red maple* is also very good.

Birch trees grow beautifully shaped forks, and the tiny, dark-colored branches are among the best for whittling miniature figures. The pith of even the smallest twigs is extremely small. Fresh birch tends to split as it dries, so let it dry for several days before beginning to work.

Oak is good, provided that you work with it before it gets too dried out.

Apple, *plum*, and *cherry* branches are especially easy to get during pruning season. You might also try branches from other fruit trees.

Poplar is good for some projects, but as the outer bark has a tendency to crack and peel when it dries, this variety of wood is not as good as maple for making roosters.

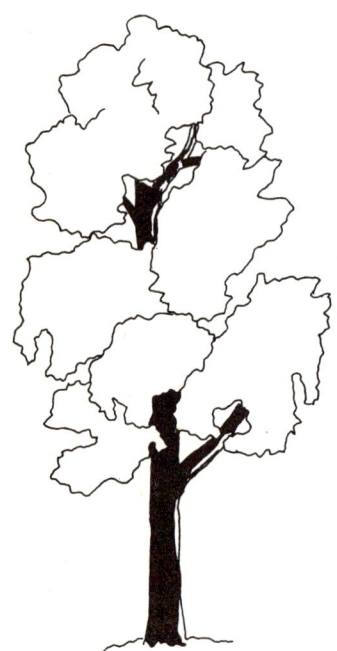

Fig. 13. Harder wood generally comes from broadleaf trees, such as elm or maple.

All About Wood

Eucalyptus branches can be very good. If you let a fresh branch dry for several days and then start whittling, you'll get very good results. Completely dry branches tend to be too brittle to produce good rooster tails, and very fresh, wet branches split as they dry. Working with eucalyptus is tricky, and you have to experiment a bit.

Pine, cedar, spruce, and other evergreens tend to violate one or more of the guidelines, but don't rule them out. You may find a branch that is perfect for one of your projects. For instance, the trunk of your Christmas tree can be turned into a good-looking lamp.

Fig. 14. This plaque is about 3" (7.6 cm) high.

Carving Twigs and Branches

Just keep your eyes open for all kinds of wood. An old branch lying on the side of the road or in the middle of the park may easily be all you need to produce some very interesting creations. Don't overlook collecting branches in the winter—with the leaves off the trees, the best wood forks are easy to spot.

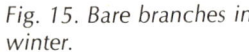

Fig. 15. Bare branches in winter.

All About Wood

SELECTING A WOOD FORK

No two wood forks are exactly alike, but the two-pronged ones do fall into several basic patterns. The best varieties for the projects in this book have one of the two top branches thicker than the other (fig. 16). For your first projects, try to avoid forks that have knots or extra branches inside the area marked by the dotted lines.

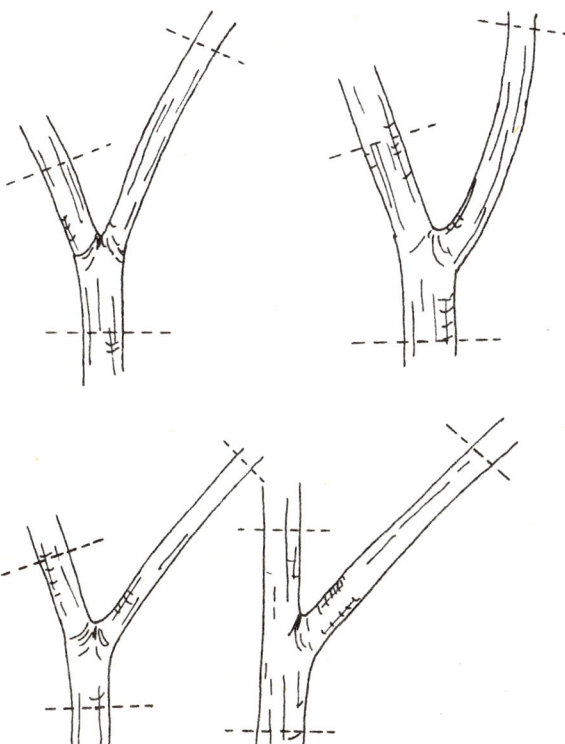

Fig. 16. You'll soon discover that each of these different varieties of wood forks has its own advantages. While all the basic shapes will lend themselves to making roosters, some will be better than others for such figures as pheasants, songbirds and horses.

21

Carving Twigs and Branches

Because of the fork's shape, the grain of the wood runs in two or three directions from the center (fig. 17). This feature provides structural strength and is one of the greatest differences between a branch figure and one carved out of a simple block of wood, in which the grain runs basically in one direction (fig. 18). Because of this, these delicate-looking animals are extremely sturdy. Finally, inasmuch as so much of the rough shaping occurs naturally, it is much easier to do this kind of carving than to carve from woodblocks.

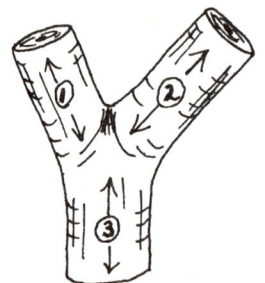

Fig. 17. The y-shape of the wood fork contributes to a final product that is strong and not easily broken, in spite of its delicate appearance. You'll be amazed at the sturdiness of your creations.

Fig. 18. Carving from a block of wood is much more complicated than carving from a wood fork.

CUTTING

There are several ways to use a knife. These methods are described and illustrated for right-handed people. Lefties should follow the illustrations and instructions, reversing the hands.

STRAIGHTAWAY CUTTING

This is good for removing a lot of unwanted wood or bark quickly. Hold the wood in your left hand and cut away from yourself with your right hand, using long strokes.

Fig. 19.

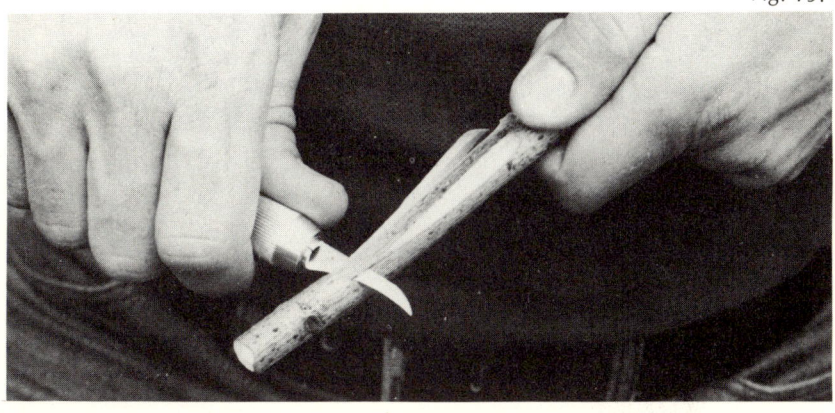

Carving Twigs and Branches

DRAWCUTTING

Here's a technique that involves placing the wood in your left hand and the knife in your right. Cut toward yourself, using short strokes. Use your right thumb as a brace against the wood.

Fig. 20.

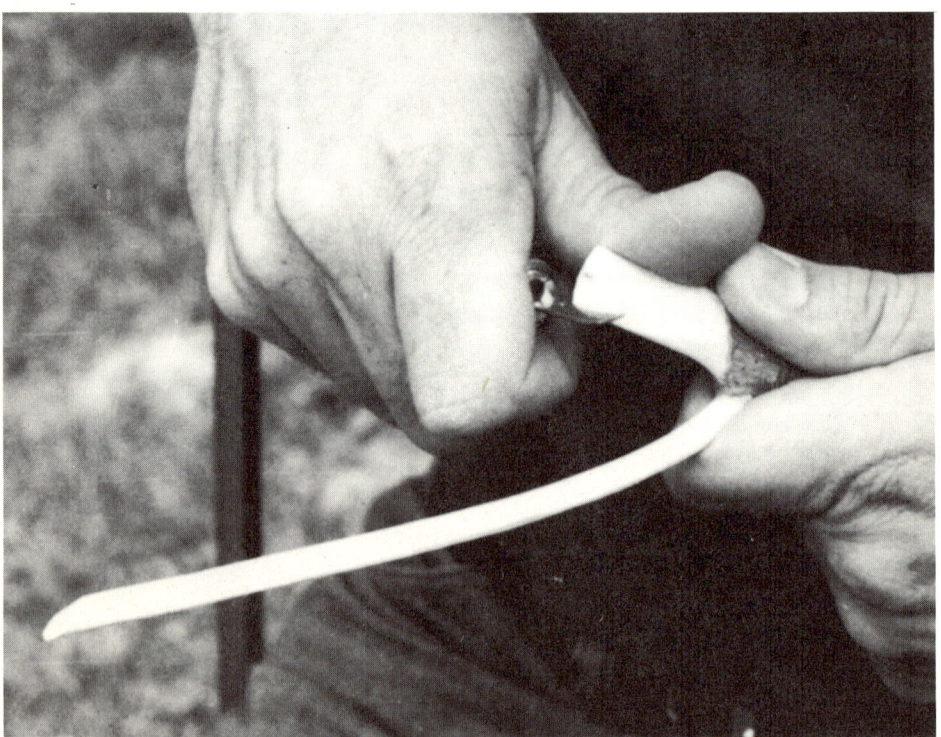

THUMBPUSHING

This is very practical for small cuts where precise control is needed. Hold the wood in the four fingers of your left hand, leaving your left thumb free. Grip the knife in your right hand, with your right thumb against the back of the blade. With your left thumb, push either the back of the blade or the back of your right thumb.

Fig. 21.

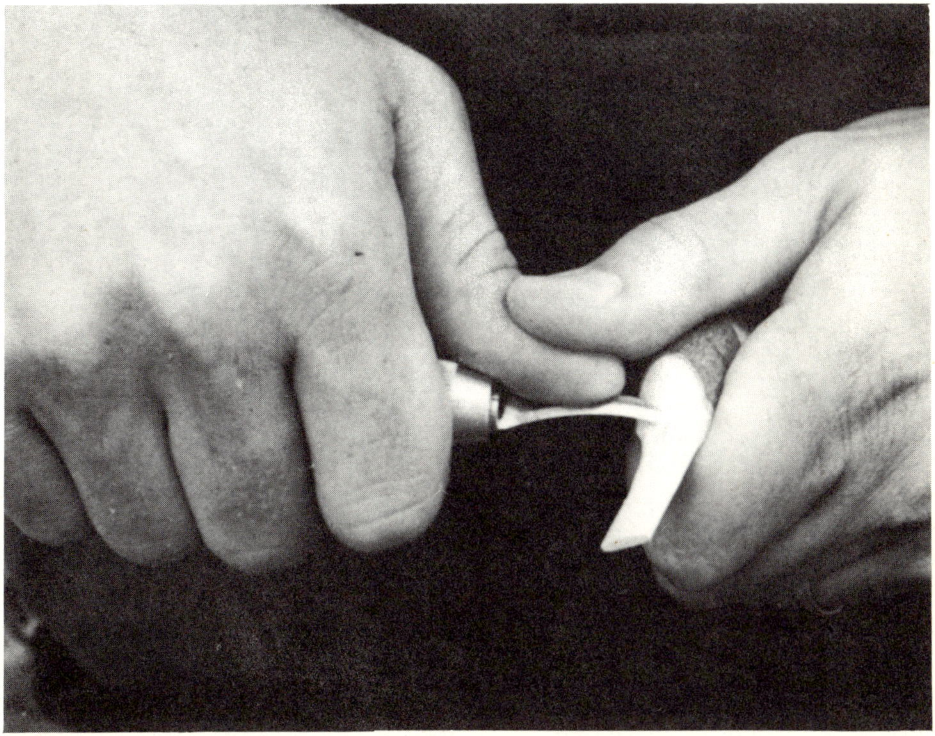

Carving Twigs and Branches

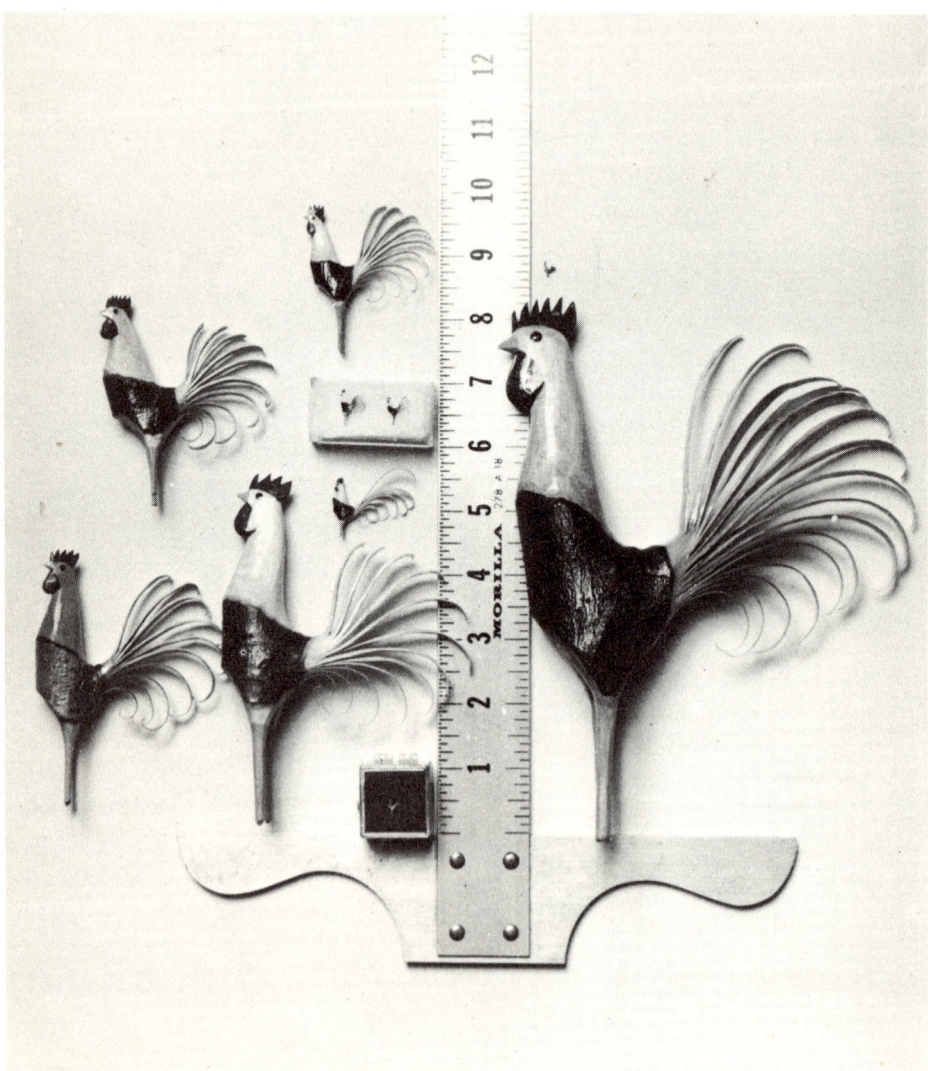

Fig. 22. This display of roosters suggests the wide variety of branch sizes you can use.

5

THE ROOSTER

The size and shape of the rooster depend largely on the thickness of the wood and the angle of the branches. Select a fork with the bottom branch between ½″ (12.70 mm) and ¾″ (19 mm) thick. After you've made several figures, you may discover some different techniques that are easier for you than those suggested here. However, for your first few roosters, follow the instructions carefully. Beginners who try to take shortcuts almost inevitably get poor results, while those who follow the instructions are almost guaranteed success on the first or second try! If you work with a penknife, you'll need both the large and small blades. If you plan to use an X-Acto knife, use blade #0101 or blade #0105 unless otherwise indicated.

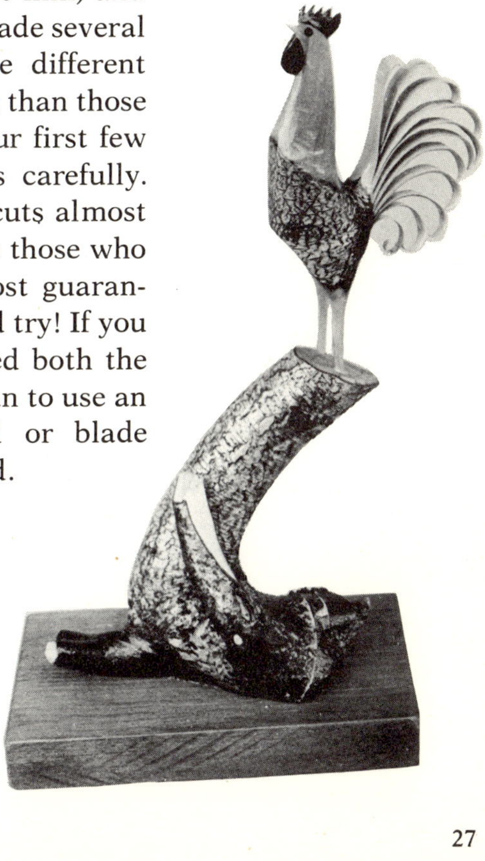

Fig. 23.

Carving Twigs and Branches

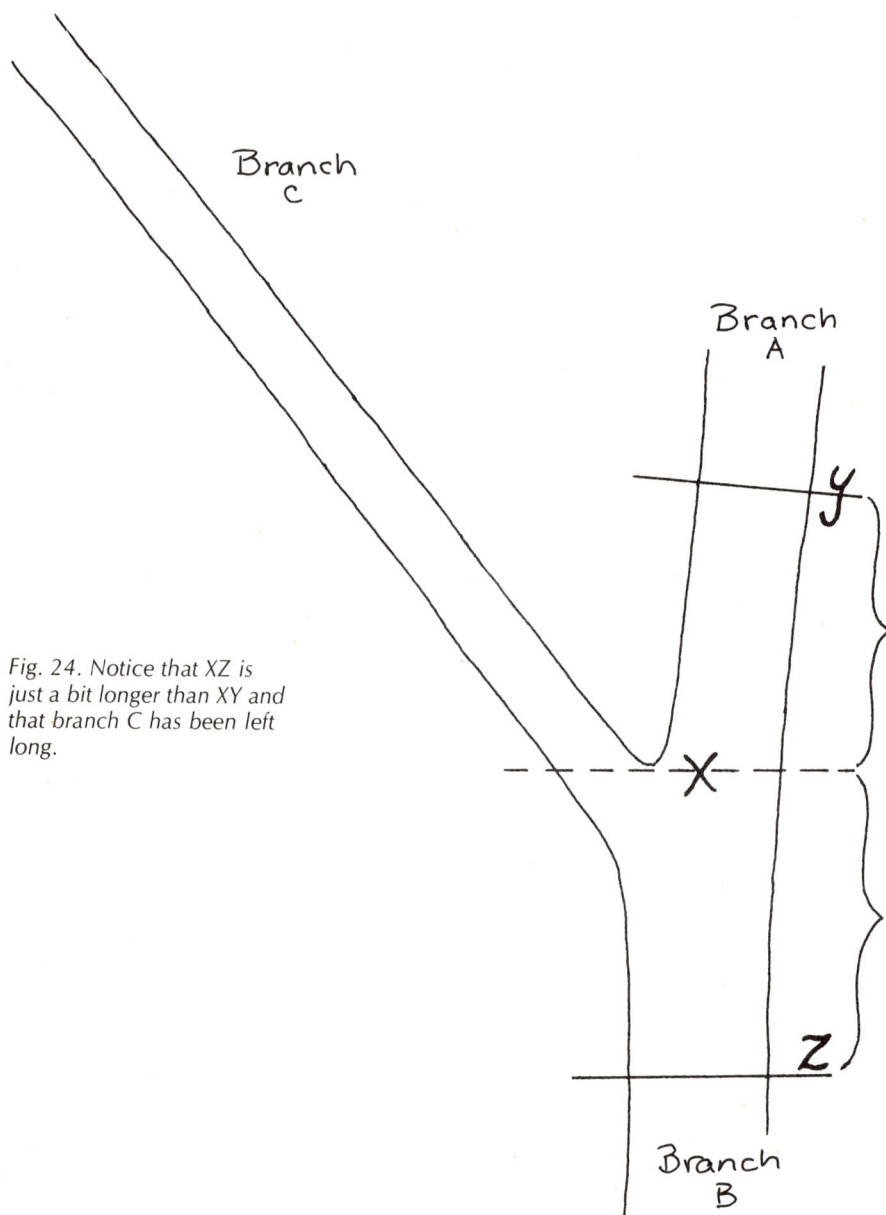

Fig. 24. Notice that XZ is just a bit longer than XY and that branch C has been left long.

28

The Rooster

MAKING THE ROOSTER

Step #1: Clean the branch with a damp cloth to remove dust and dirt. Dirt on the wood or on your hands will cause your work to look smudgy.

Step #2: Cut branch A (head) and branch B (legs) to the proper length. Leave branch C (tail) about 6″ (15 cm) or 7″ (18 cm) long. It's important that you leave the tail branch longer than the ones for the head and legs. The length of the head branch is just slightly shorter than the branch for the legs. The length of the head branch is 2-2½ times its own thickness. If you want to make a stockier rooster, shorten the branches for the head and legs. A tall, thin rooster would require longer branches for the head and legs.

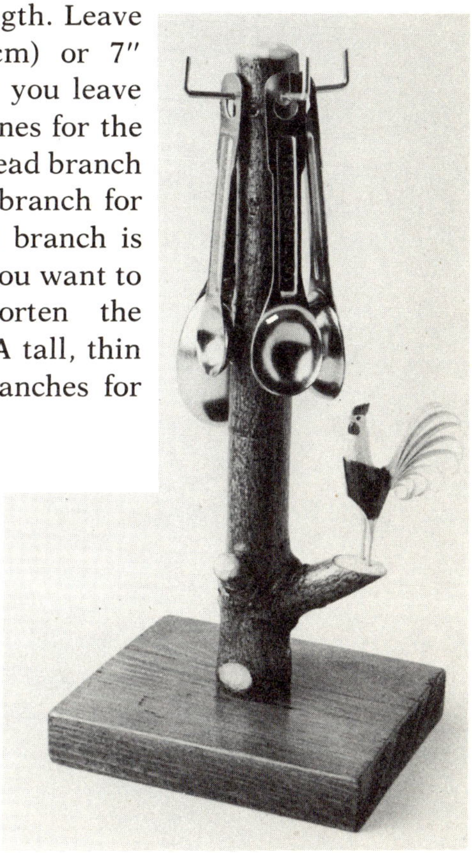

Fig. 25. This kitchen-utensil tree came from a discarded maple branch and a scrap of board found under a lumberyard workbench.

Carving Twigs and Branches

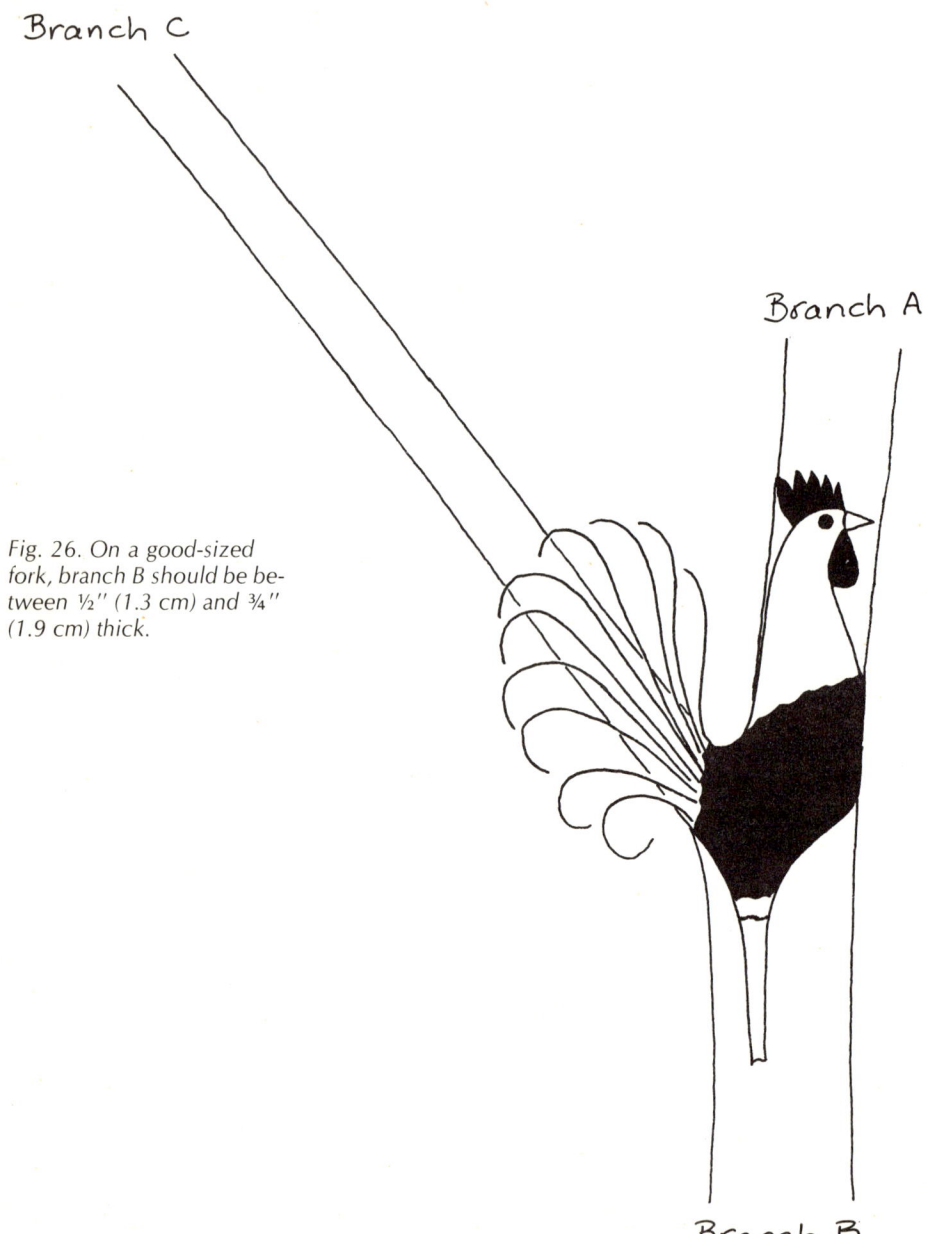

Fig. 26. On a good-sized fork, branch B should be between ½" (1.3 cm) and ¾" (1.9 cm) thick.

The Rooster

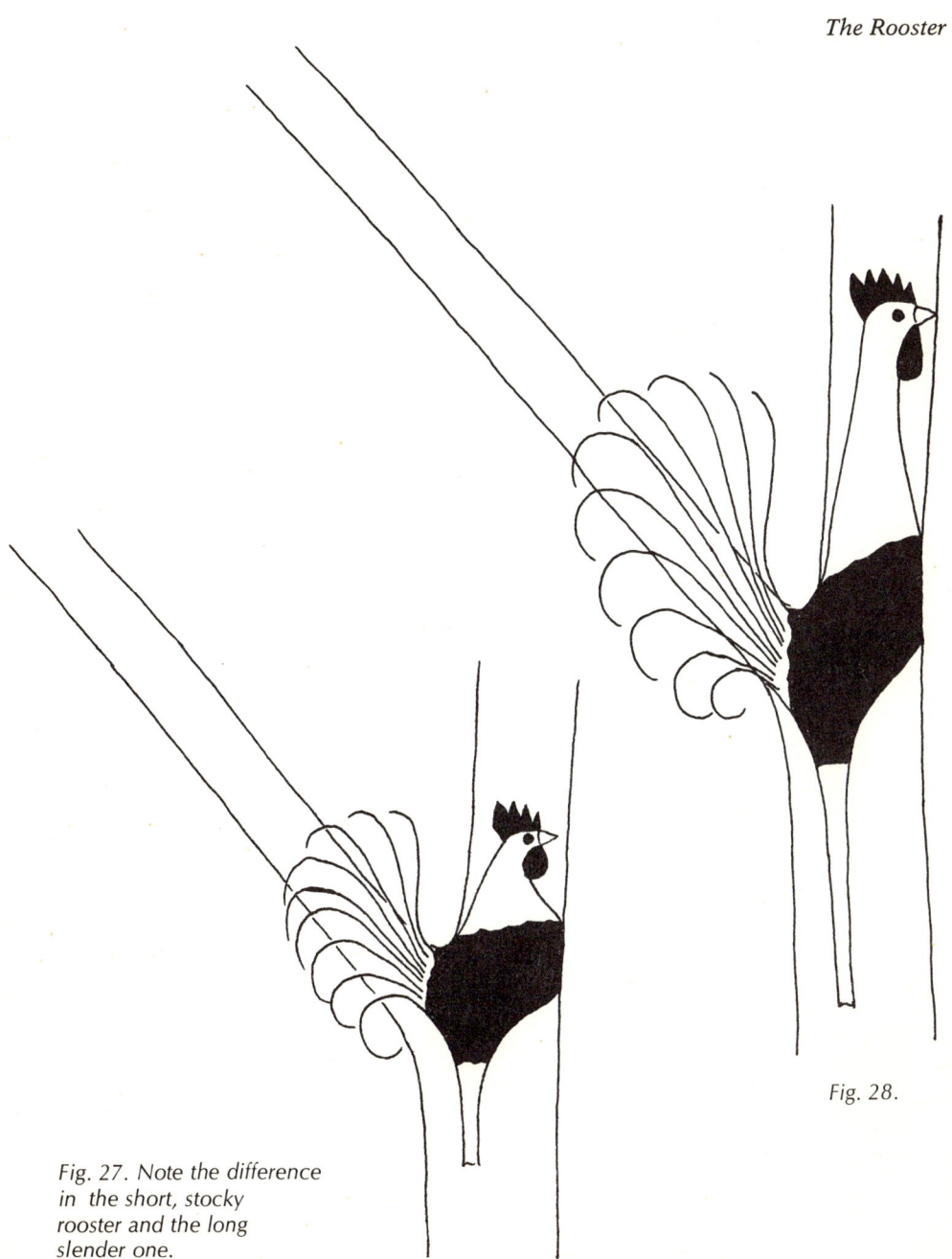

Fig. 27. Note the difference in the short, stocky rooster and the long slender one.

Fig. 28.

Carving Twigs and Branches

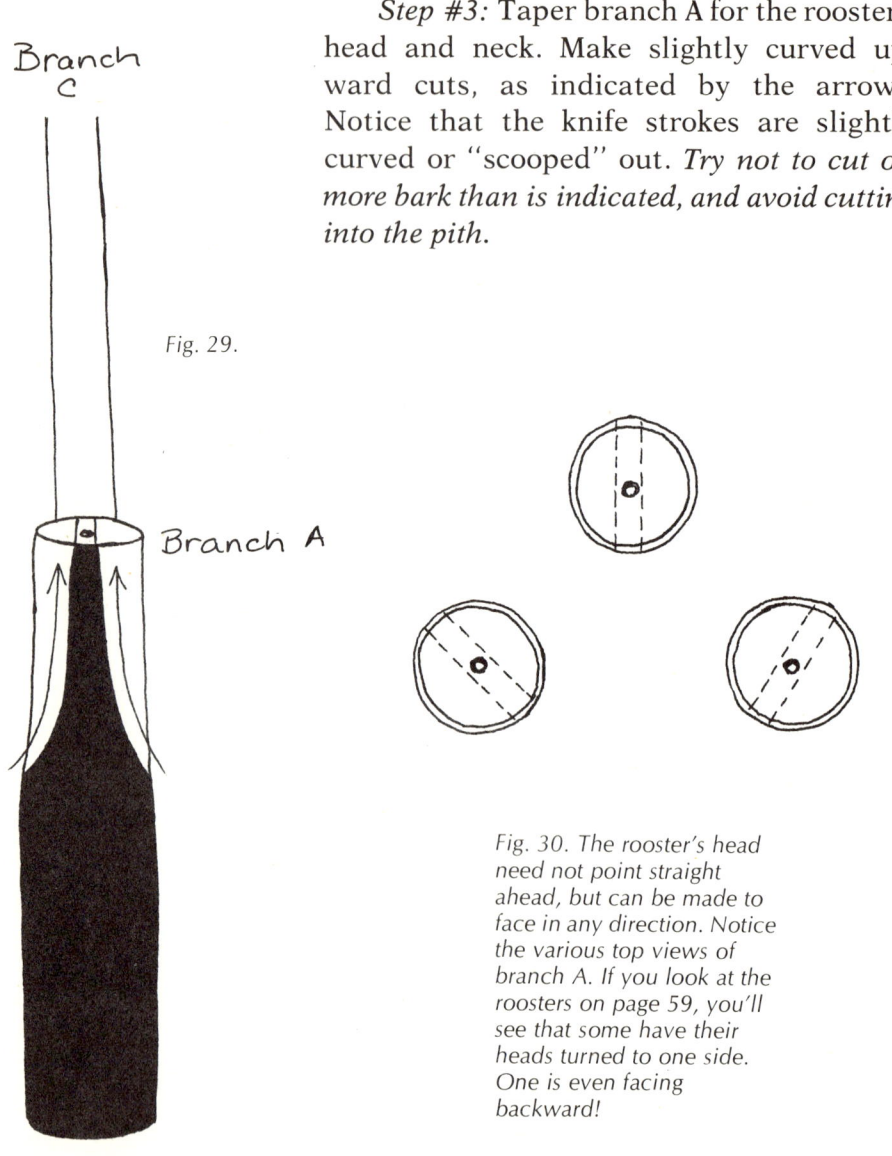

Step #3: Taper branch A for the rooster's head and neck. Make slightly curved upward cuts, as indicated by the arrows. Notice that the knife strokes are slightly curved or "scooped" out. *Try not to cut off more bark than is indicated, and avoid cutting into the pith.*

Fig. 29.

Fig. 30. The rooster's head need not point straight ahead, but can be made to face in any direction. Notice the various top views of branch A. If you look at the roosters on page 59, you'll see that some have their heads turned to one side. One is even facing backward!

The Rooster

Step #4: Taper branch B for the rooster's legs. Note where the cuts for making the legs start in relation to the fork. If you want the rooster's chest to puff out more, make the front cut deeper than the back cut. The more you take off the front of branch B, the more the rooster's chest will stand out. You *will* cut through the pith in this step.

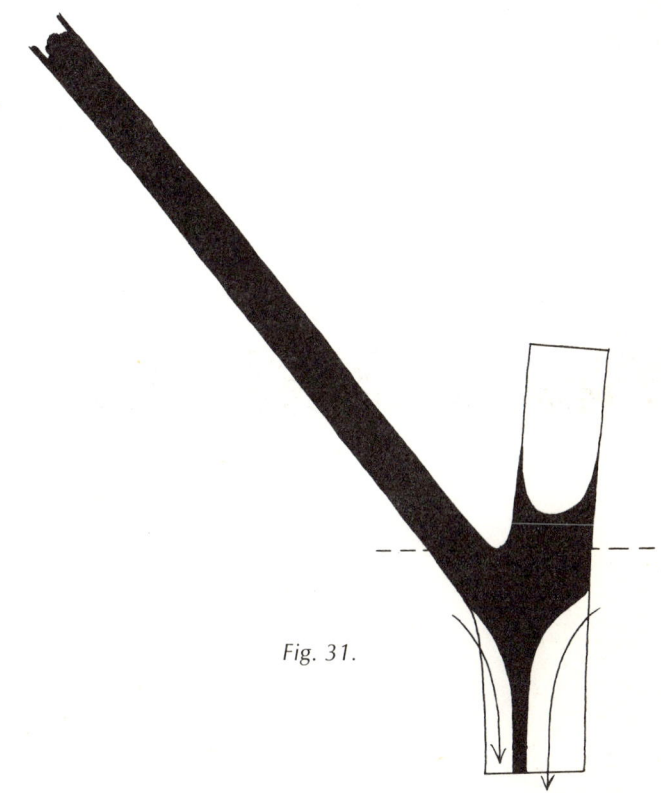

Fig. 31.

33

Carving Twigs and Branches

Step #5: Shave the bark off branches A, B, and C, as indicated in fig. 32. The rooster's bark "vest" should remain after this step. Notice how it curves upward from back to front. Be careful not to shave off too much of the wood underneath.

Fig. 32.

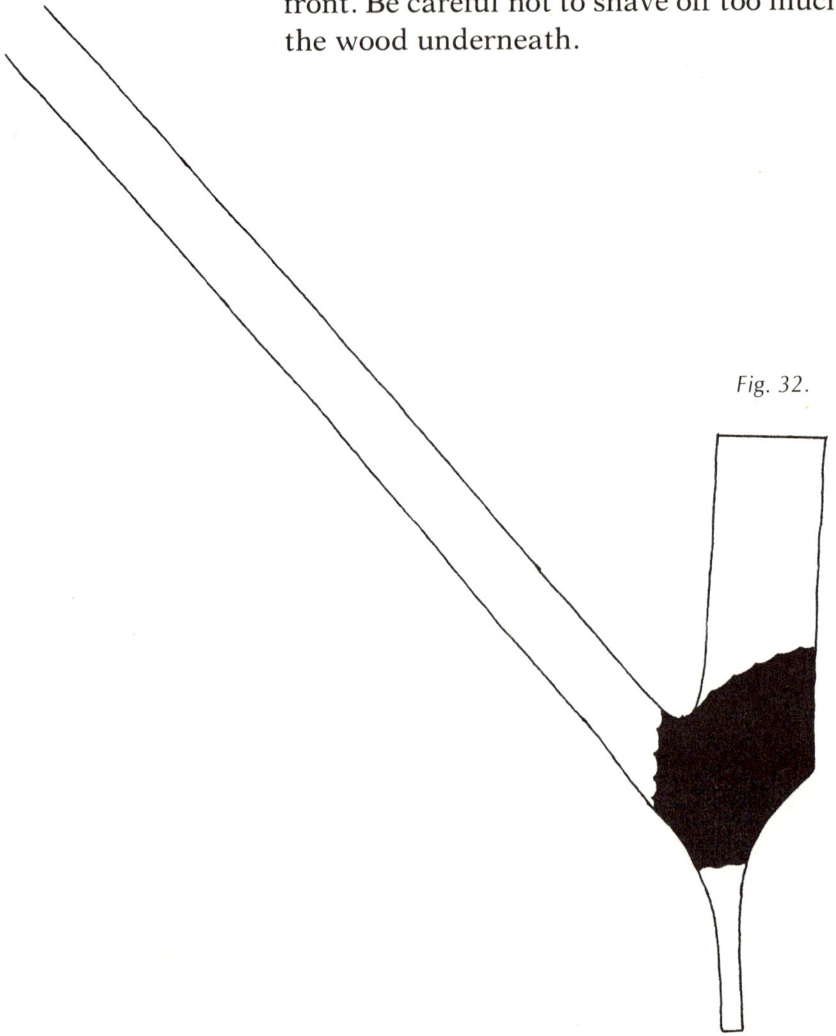

The Rooster

Step #6: Form the legs by cutting away the area marked with an "X" (fig. 34). Make upward v-cuts, using a penknife or X-Acto blades #0101, #0105, or #27, or cut downward, using the point of your penknife or X-Acto blades #24 or #0105. (Cut from the asterisk.) An alternative method is to drill a hole through the point marked with the asterisk and then cut upward toward the hole. (See fig. 33.) This last method is the easiest way to remove the excess wood from larger roosters.

Fig. 33.

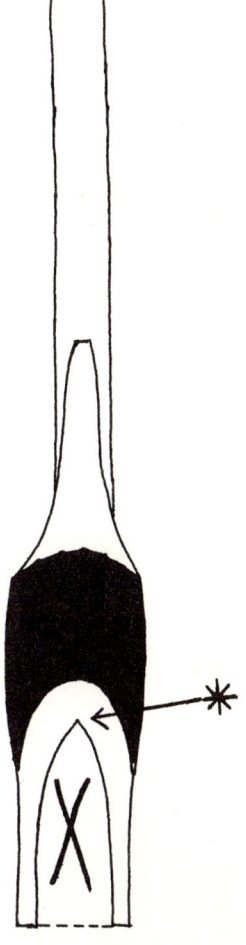

Fig. 34. Follow the arrows to make your cuts. Do the same, front and back, until you have removed the wood marked by the X.

Carving Twigs and Branches

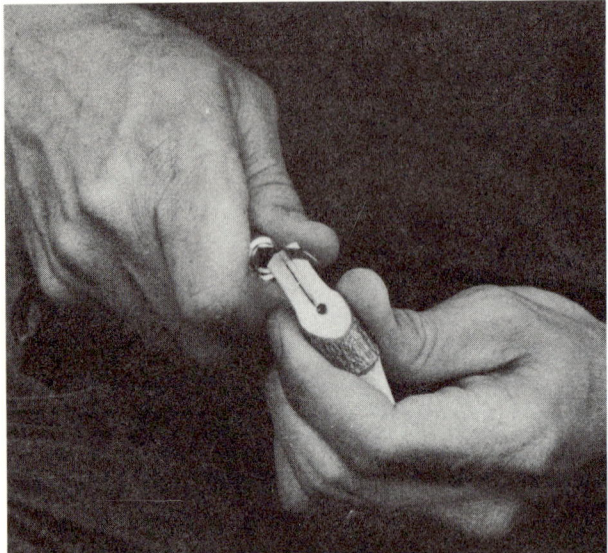

Fig. 35. Removing the wood to form the rooster's legs.

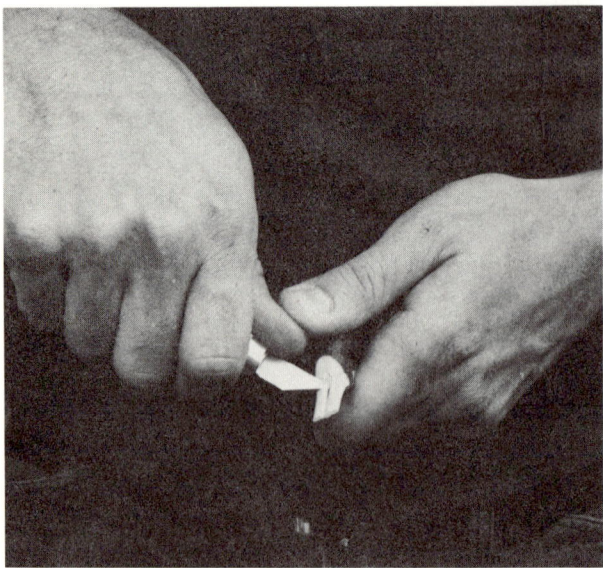

Fig. 36.

Step #7: Round and smooth the legs, using a fine-point blade like X-Acto #24 or #0105. To smooth away any rough spots, you can sand this area with a piece of sandpaper wrapped around either a nail or thin twig.

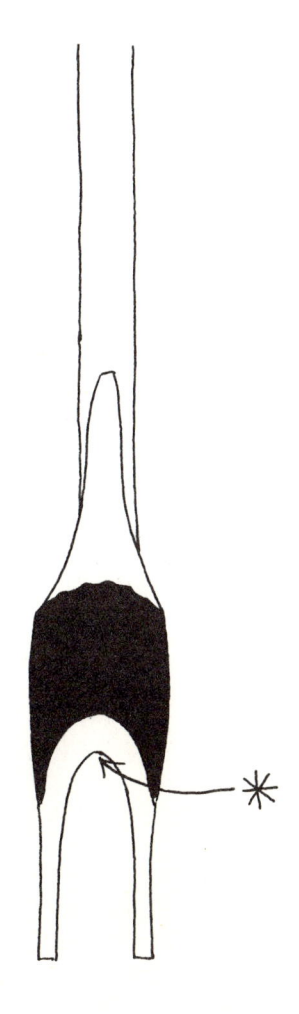

Fig. 37. Sand this area.

Carving Twigs and Branches

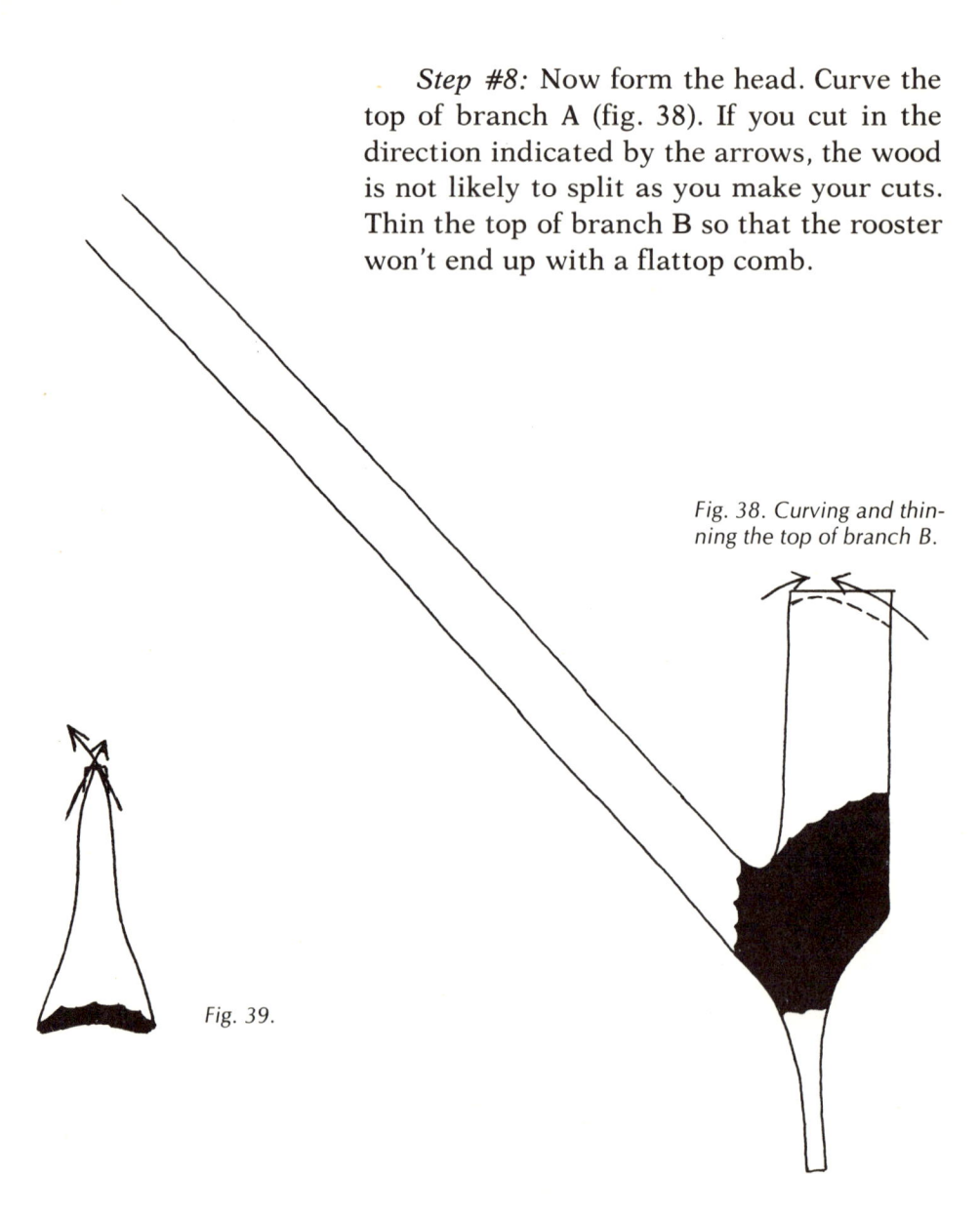

Step #8: Now form the head. Curve the top of branch A (fig. 38). If you cut in the direction indicated by the arrows, the wood is not likely to split as you make your cuts. Thin the top of branch B so that the rooster won't end up with a flattop comb.

Fig. 38. Curving and thinning the top of branch B.

Fig. 39.

38

The Rooster

You may find it quite helpful at this point to sketch the entire head lightly before going on. Take your pattern from the photo shown here. Carve the top of the rooster's comb, beginning at the back. The first cut angles downward toward the front of the rooster. The second comes straight down, following the grain of the wood. Make these cuts very carefully. Be sure not to twist the knife blade, and not to press down too hard. The number of teeth on the comb may vary from rooster to rooster, depending upon how wide you make each one and the thickness of the branch.

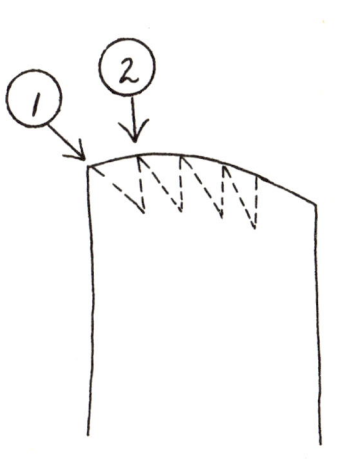

Fig. 41. Carving the rooster's comb.

Fig. 40. Sketch the rooster's head from this pattern. This rooster might look a little "blah" now, but a few dabs of paint will just about make him wake up and crow!

Carving Twigs and Branches

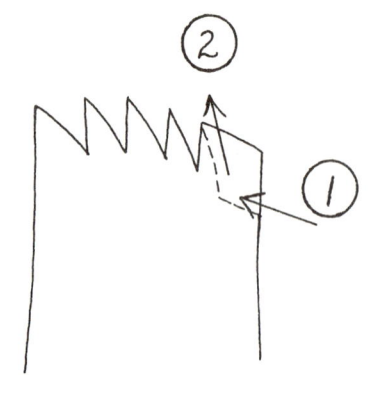

Fig. 42. Begin forming the beak.

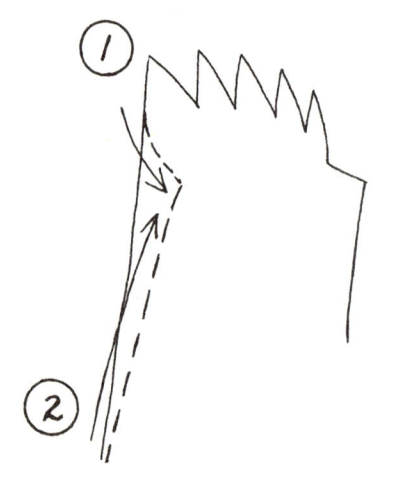

Fig. 43. Finish the comb and taper the back of the neck.

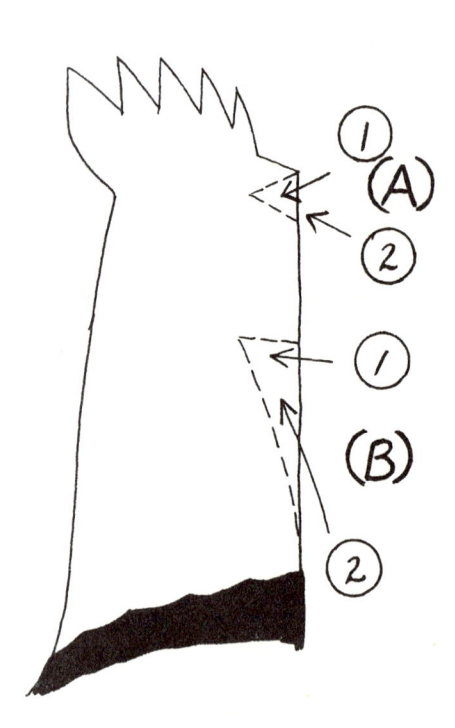

Fig. 44. Shape the beak, wattles, and front of the neck.

40

The Rooster

Shape the top of the beak and the front tooth of the comb. You can twist the knife blade upward without splitting the wood when you make the second cut.

Cut the back point of the comb, and taper and round off the back of the rooster's neck. Take your time. Don't try to do this step in just two strokes.

Shape the rooster's beak, wattles, and front of the neck. (See fig. 44.) Cut the beak first (A), then the wattles, and then the front of the neck (B). When you have had a little practice, try making a crowing rooster with its beak open. (See figs. 45 and 46.) Sharpen the rooster's beak slightly.

Fig. 45. Crowing rooster.

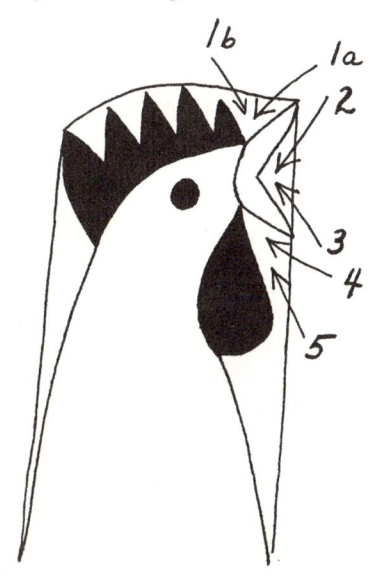

Fig. 46. Rooster with its beak open.

41

Carving Twigs and Branches

Round off the wattles and the front of the neck. Split the wattles by making a thin vertical v-cut with the point of your blade for a more realistic rooster.

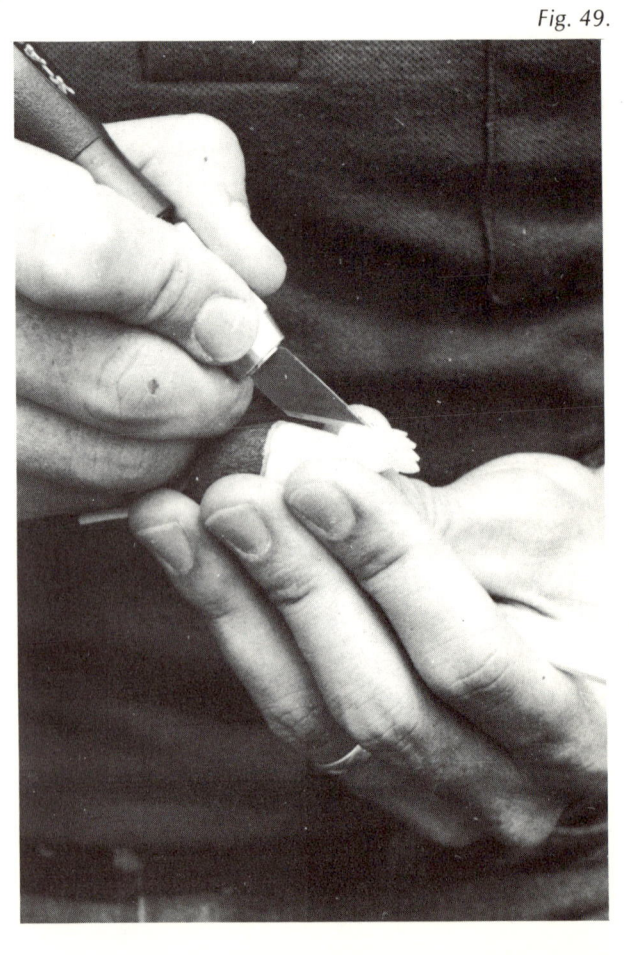

Fig. 47. Rounding and splitting the wattles.

Fig. 48.

Fig. 49.

The Rooster

Step #9: Form the tail using X-Acto blade #26. With a little practice and some concentration, this will become one of the easiest steps. Remember, if you are using a freshly cut branch, it should first be allowed to dry for a day or two after you have removed the bark, so the tail feathers will curl when you make the cuts. Try making a few practice tails on other sticks before doing your rooster's tail.

Fig. 50. Do a few practice tails before attempting the tail on your first rooster.

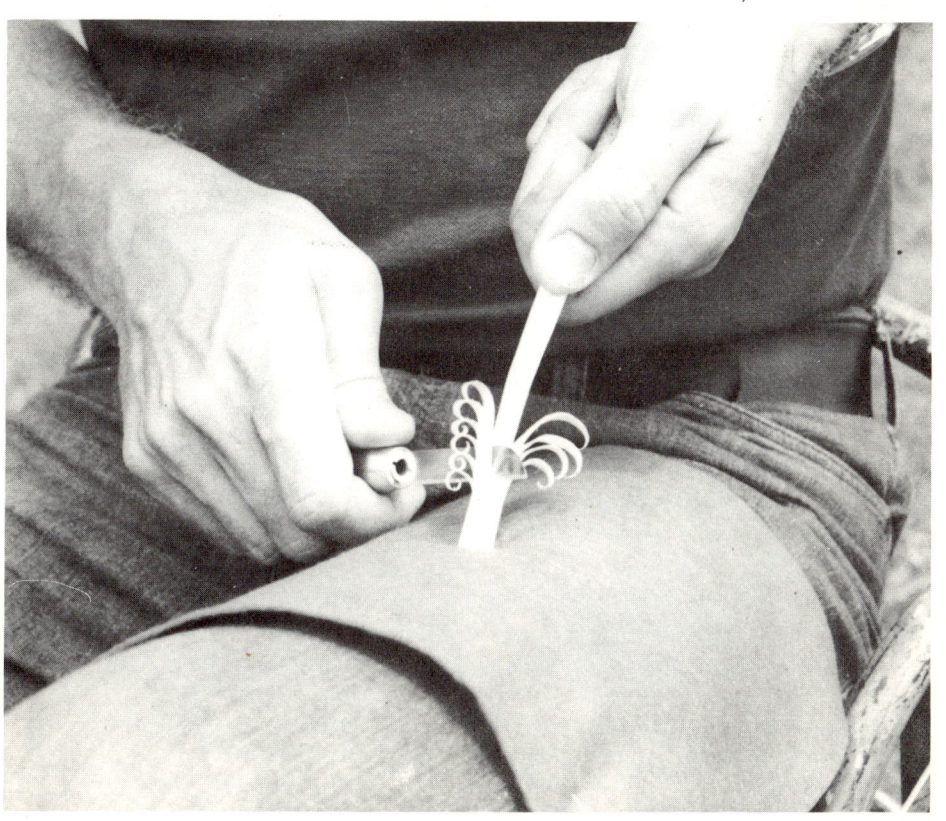

Carving Twigs and Branches

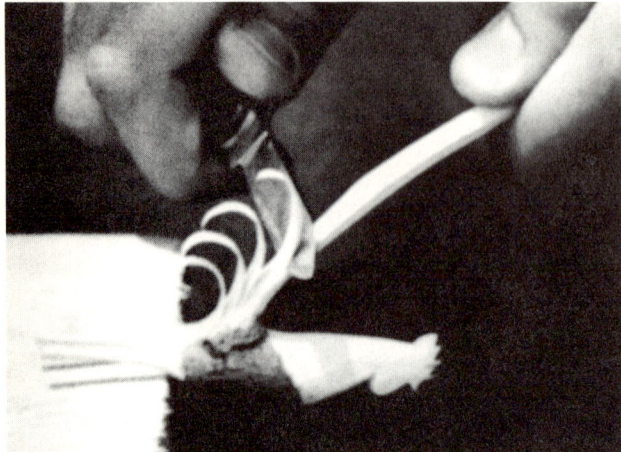

Fig. 51. Pretend that you're trying to slice a two-pound roast thin enough to serve sixty!

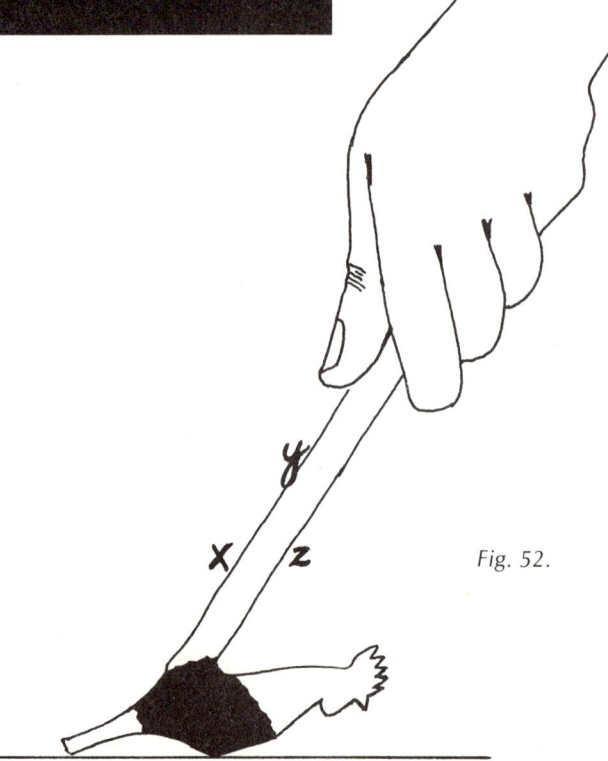

Fig. 52.

44

The Rooster

Rest the rooster's chest and legs against a table or block or against your leg. You may want to put a piece of heavy cloth or leather between the rooster and your leg. Using a forward motion, start slicing downward from point X on the branch, keeping the blade almost flat against the wood and slicing thinly.

Start each new feather a bit higher up, until you have what you feel should be the longest one of the tail, point Y. Then cut each one a little shorter until you reach point Z. The number of feathers you end up with depends on how thin each feather is and how much wood you have to work with. There is no rule about how many feathers your rooster has to have, so don't worry if you slice off a few in the process.

Fig. 53. Slicing the tail feathers.

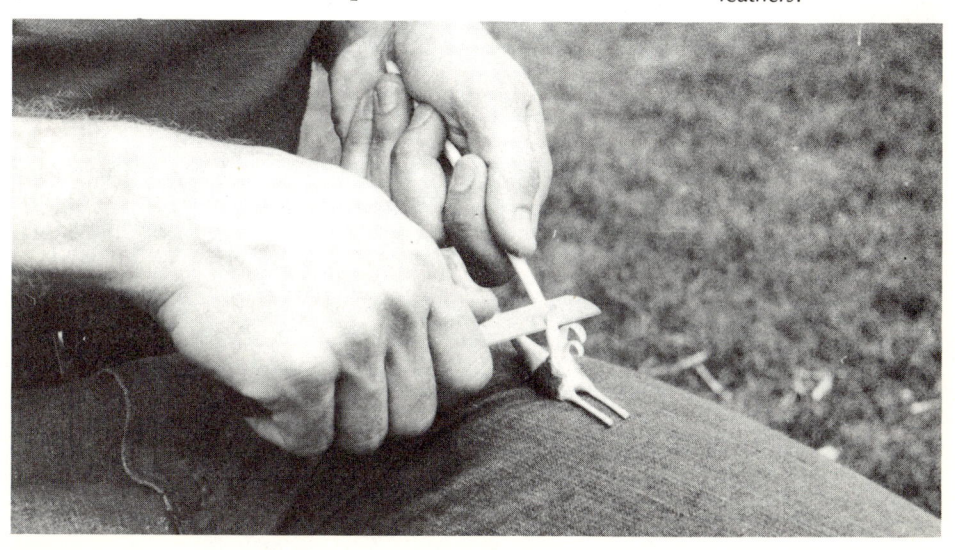

Carving Twigs and Branches

Fig. 54. Using the flat part of the knife to spread the tail feathers apart.

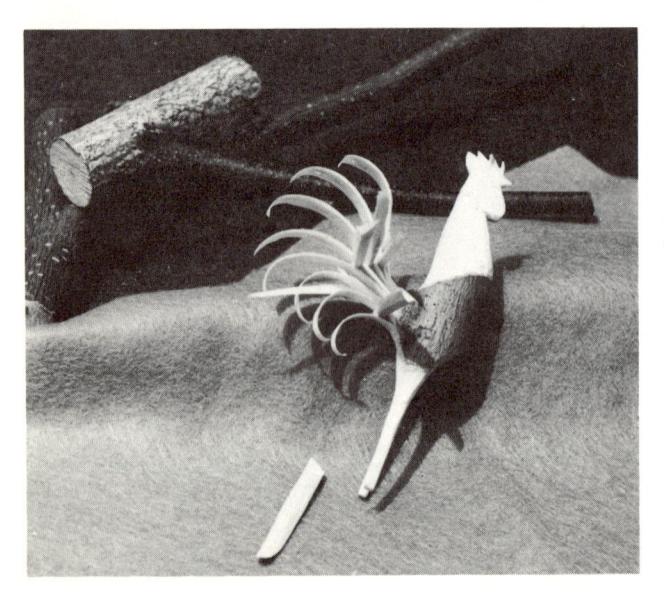

Fig. 55. Wedging wood chips in between the feathers.

The Rooster

If branch C is somewhat dry when you make the tail, the feathers will curl beautifully by themselves if you slice them thinly enough. You can get some of them to curl even more by bending and shaping them carefully with your fingers. This is especially true of the first few feathers.

You can also make the whole tail fan out by bending the feathers apart. There are two ways to do this. You can use the flat part of your knife blade to spread the individual feathers apart, or you can wedge little wood chips between the feathers. The tail will set completely in an hour or so.

In order for the last tail feather (the one closest to the back of the rooster's neck) to bend more easily in the direction indicated in fig. 56, you may want to thin the base a little, as the bottom part of this feather does tend to be a bit thick. The part you may want to thin is indicated by the asterisk, and the direction of your cutting at this point should be from the base of the feather toward the tip.

Fig. 56. Bending the tail feathers apart.

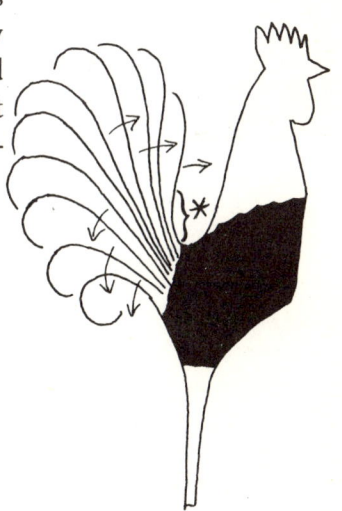

Carving Twigs and Branches

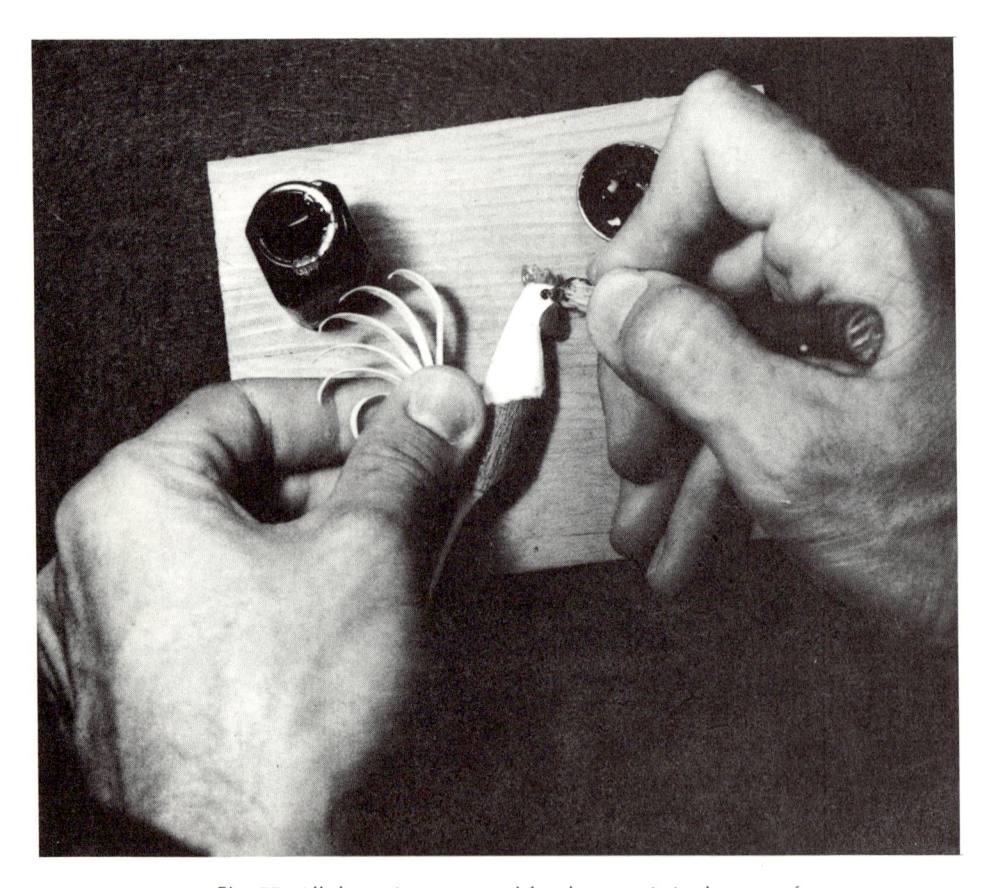

Fig. 57. All the paint you need for the eyes is in the cap of the paint jar. After shaking the jar, leaving the cap off for a few minutes will allow the paint to become thick enough not to bleed down the grain of the wood.

The Rooster

Step #10: Smooth any rough spots and round off any unwanted corners or angles, using either your knife or a small piece of sandpaper. Then paint and finish your rooster. For the comb, wattles, beak, and legs, a little paintbrush is fine, but you will have much more control in painting the eyes if you use a toothpick or a small sharpened stick. Make sure that the paint is thick enough not to bleed into the wood. Leaving the cap off the jar for a few minutes will allow the paint in the cap to become the right consistency.

If you want more detailed eyes, you can paint a black dot and let it dry. Then paint a slightly smaller yellow dot in the middle of the black one. When the yellow dot is dry, place a smaller black dot in the center of the yellow one.

Fig. 58. Pheasant with detailed eyes.

Carving Twigs and Branches

Step #11: Make a stand for the rooster. Choose a nice fork for the stand. Using a nail or other sharp instrument, put two holes in your stand for the rooster's legs. Glue the rooster in place.

Fig. 59. Some stands you can make.

The Rooster

Step #12: Now, if you wish, finish your project with either shellac or polyurethane. Shellac is fine for use with dry wood in a dry atmosphere, but it will take most of the curl out of a rooster's tail in humid weather. Clear polyurethane takes longer to dry than shellac, but it won't affect the curl, even in extremely humid conditions. It also provides a more durable finish. If you have both shellac and polyurethane handy, you may want to use shellac for the stand and polyurethane for the rooster.

Fig. 60. Some sawed-off stumps and fallen logs can add a lot to a set of candle holders. Use a brace and bit or an electric drill with a wood bit to make the hole for the candle.

Carving Twigs and Branches

CORRECTING MISTAKES

If your knife slips and you spoil a rooster by miscutting the comb, beak, or legs, don't throw the branch away. There are several ways to salvage it.

If you spoil the head, just cut it off and start over again. Make a stockier rooster, shortening the legs as well.

If you slice off part of the rooster's legs, you can shorten branch A slightly and make a smaller rooster, or you can make a hen or a baby chick.

Another alternative is to invert the fork and shorten branches A and B. Make the rooster's legs into ears or horns, paint eyes and a mouth, and you have the head or neck of a horse, giraffe, or goat. For the giraffe or goat, make separate ears and glue them into the side of the head, since the rooster's legs have been converted into horns.

If you break off a beak or the back tip of the comb, or if you split the rooster's head a little, don't be afraid to use a dab of glue to stick the broken piece on again or reinforce a weak part.

Fig. 61. You can make this horse penholder from what would have been a rooster.

The Rooster

A FINAL WORD ABOUT THE ROOSTER

While it isn't the easiest thing to carve from a wood fork, it does make you familiar with all the basic techniques you need to know in order to make everything else in this book. Once you get the hang of it, you'll probably be making roosters from start to finish in no more than twenty to thirty minutes!

Fig. 62. This candle holder is 9¼" (23.5 cm) from the bottom of the base to the top of the rooster's comb.

Carving Twigs and Branches

Fig. 63. The tremendous variety of shapes that exist in little "stumps," twigs, and branches provides all kinds of settings for your figures. The main things you need are wide-open eyes and a good imagination.

6

OTHER PROJECTS

For all the following projects, use the same basic techniques used in creating the rooster. You can add a tremendous amount of interest to your branch animals by placing them on different stands and in different settings. In this chapter a great number of stands are shown, all of them incorporating branches and twigs of many different shapes and sizes. Twigs and branches as they are found in nature offer infinite creative possibilities. All you need is a little imagination.

If you don't have any scraps of wood around the house, you can get some at a lumberyard. Scraps of wood that are thrown away are perfect for mounting your figures. Access to a drill and saw can greatly expand the variety of your projects.

Fig. 64. Scraps from the lumberyard. I don't remember ever having to pay a cent for such bits of wood. By the way, millwork is especially good to use.

Carving Twigs and Branches

AN ALBUM OF IDEAS

Remember, whatever you work on will reflect your unique design, style, and choices. How carefully you work, and also how patiently, will show up in each of your projects. With a little practice you'll create treasures large and small that you and your friends will be proud to own.

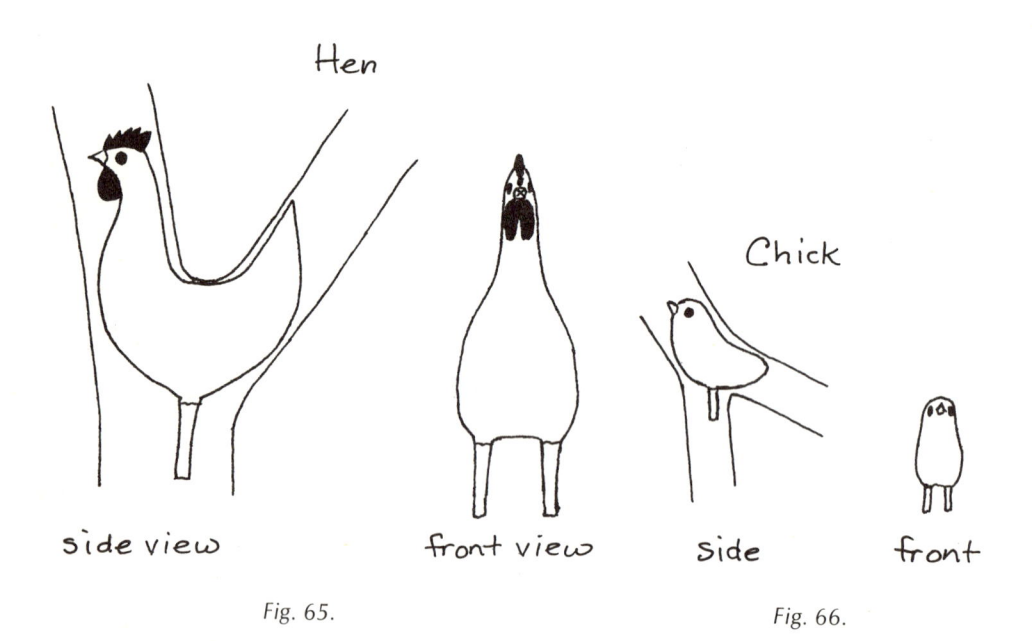

Fig. 65.

Fig. 66.

Other Projects

Hen and baby chick: Try putting a whole family together—rooster, hen, and chicks.

Fig. 67. By changing the proportions shown on the facing page, you can come up with a very chubby chicken, or one built like a champion marathon runner. In addition to the trio shown here, a whole string of little chicks following a mother hen would look pretty neat, don't you think?

57

Carving Twigs and Branches

Fig. 68. Notice the raised feathers on the fighting rooster's neck.

58

Other Projects

"People": The various shapes and stances of these roosters suggest caricatures of human reactions, temperaments, and personalities. See how many you can figure out. To make the fighting rooster's neck, ruffle the feathers, by using the tip of your blade to make little shavings.

Fig. 69.

Carving Twigs and Branches

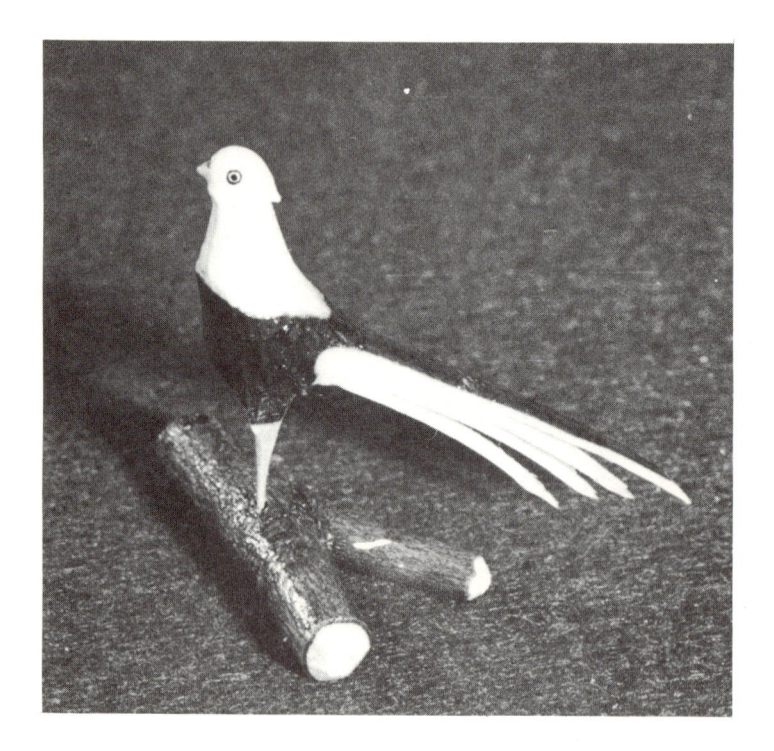

Fig. 70. Here's a pheasant before the tail feathers have been glued together. (See page 49 for an "after" shot.) Also, notice the detailed eye, made by following the technique discussed on page 49. The little feathers on the back of the head of Fig. 71 are formed by making a few shavings in the wood—sort of like an upside-down minature rooster tail. This pheasant's eye has a leaf-shaped area around it in red.

Observe the variety of heads possible. The head of Fig. 72 isn't as thin at the top as the rooster's head is. Instead of coming to a fairly thin edge, it's rounder.

Keep in mind that it's easier to whittle a pheasant when the wood is quite fresh. You don't want the tail feathers to curl. Also, be sure to leave the bark on the top of the tail.

Other Projects

Pheasants: A pheasant is one of the prettiest birds that can be carved from a forked twig. The ones pictured here are a little different from those found in nature. If you want to paint them realistically, look at a painting or photograph to get the exact markings and coloring. To make the tail on the second type of pheasant (fig. 73), slice the wood to form the feathers, then glue the feathers together. Use a rubber band or a piece of thread to hold the feathers together while the glue is drying.

Pheasant

Fig. 72.

front view

Fig. 71.

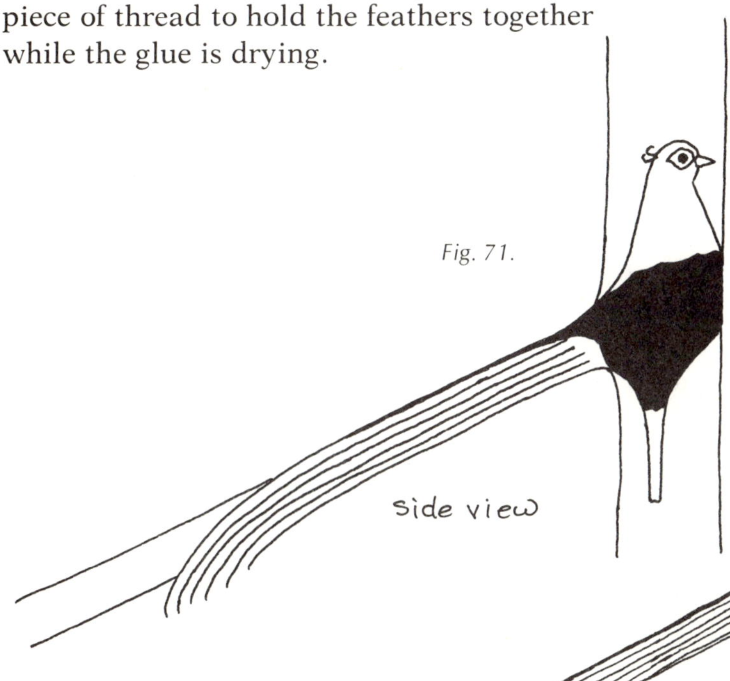

side view

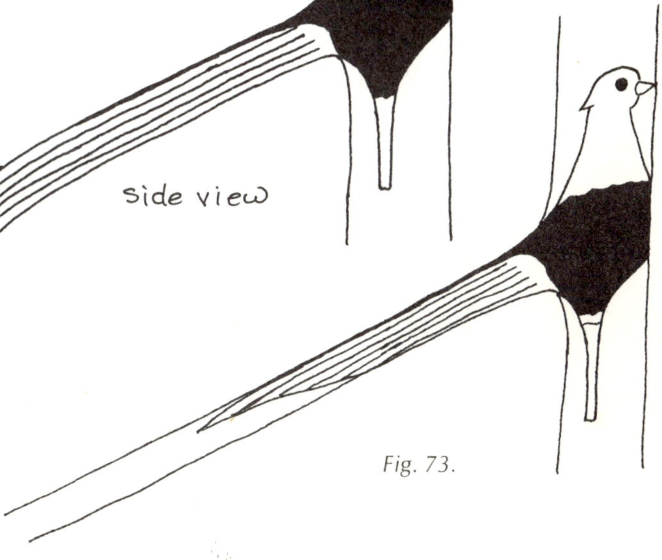

Fig. 73.

61

Heron

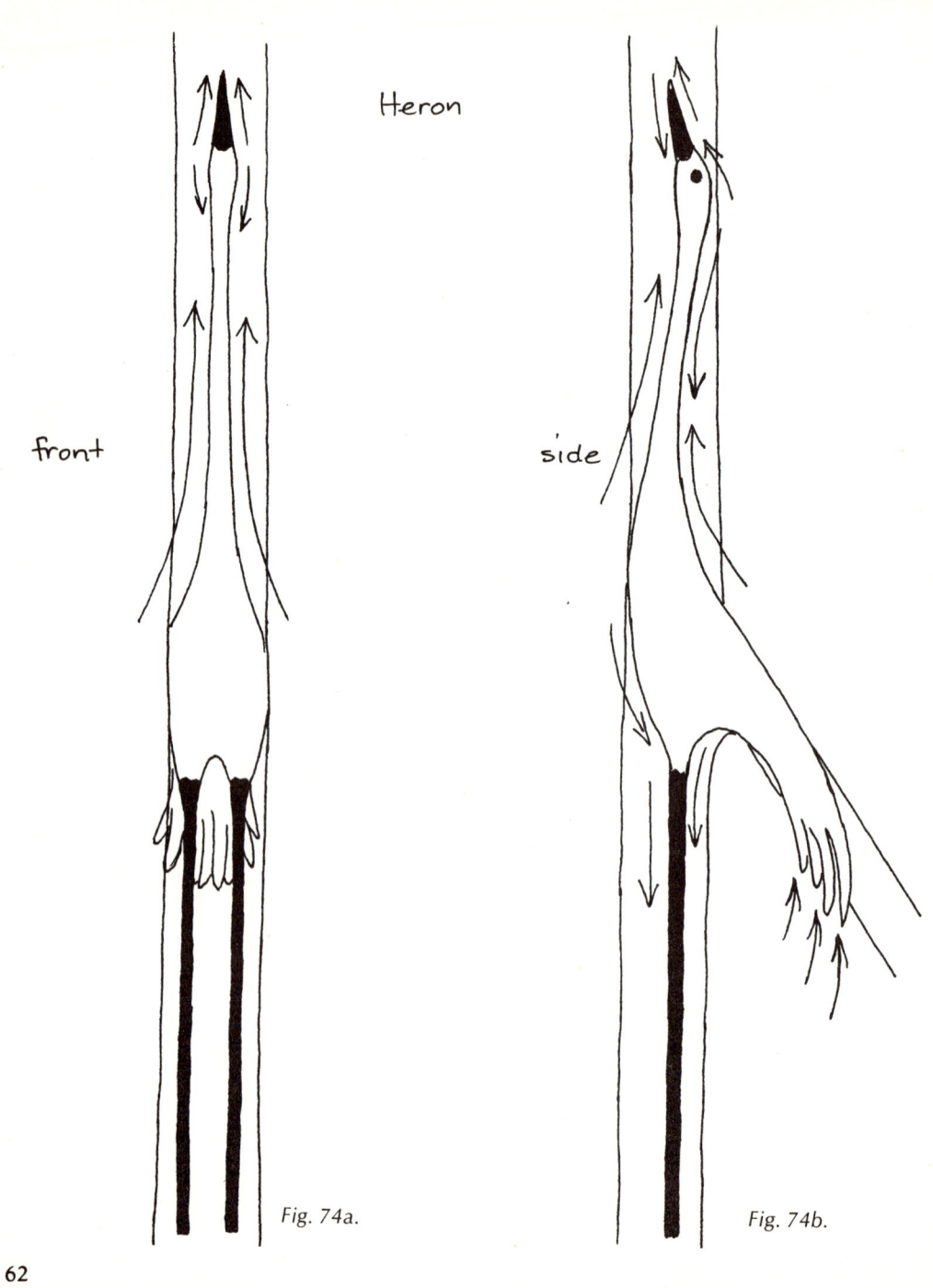

front

side

Fig. 74a.

Fig. 74b.

62

Other Projects

Heron: To make the heron, you need a fork with long and straight A and B branches. Follow the arrows in figs. 74a and 74b when you make your cuts, in order not to split the wood.

Fig. 75. These herons are made of swamp maple and are very sturdy—even with their skinny legs!

63

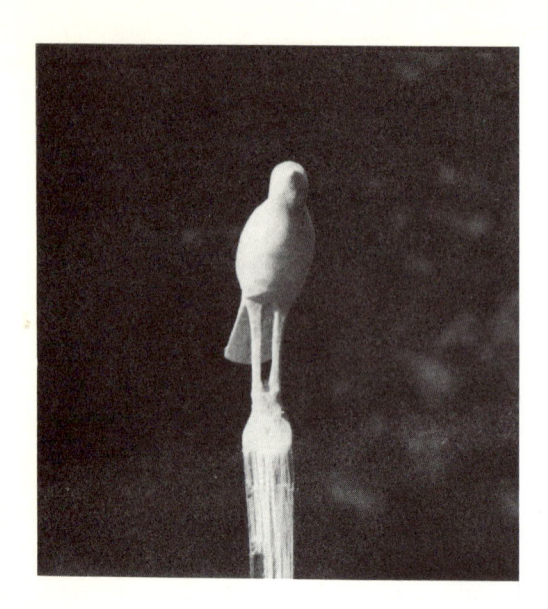

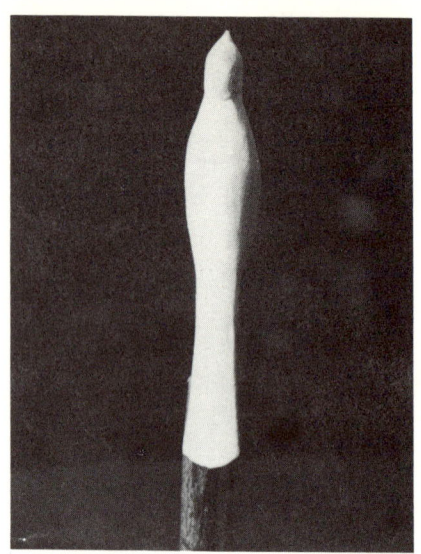

Figs. 76–79. Songbirds can be made to look up or down—depending on whether they're singing or looking for worms!

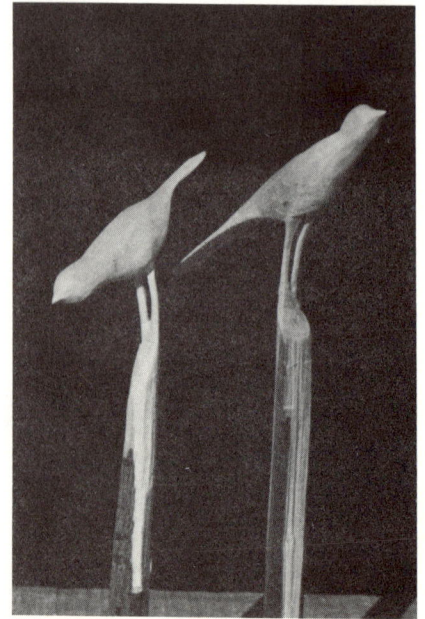

64

Water Bird

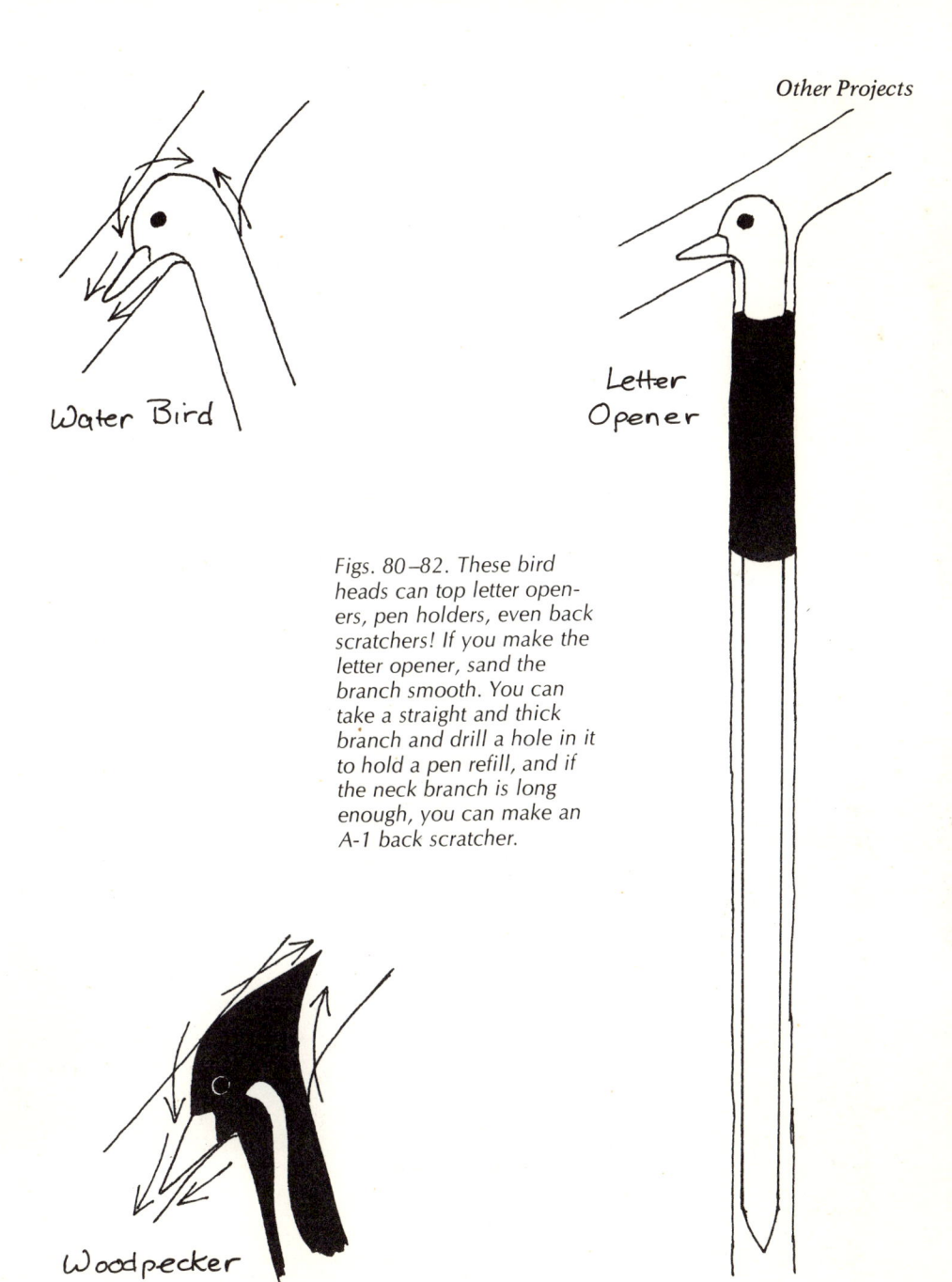

Other Projects

Letter Opener

Figs. 80–82. These bird heads can top letter openers, pen holders, even back scratchers! If you make the letter opener, sand the branch smooth. You can take a straight and thick branch and drill a hole in it to hold a pen refill, and if the neck branch is long enough, you can make an A-1 back scratcher.

Woodpecker

65

Carving Twigs and Branches

Horse, goat, and giraffe: Body, legs, and tail can be made of straight sticks cut to the proper lengths and glued together to form horse and goat. A little variation creates the giraffe.

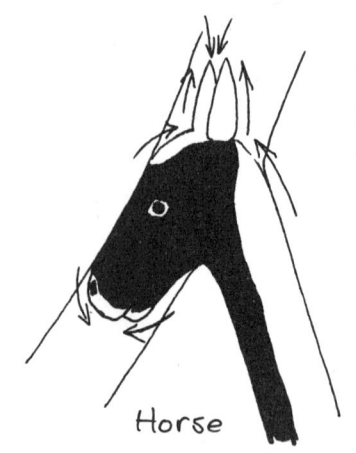

Fig. 83.

Fig. 84.

Fig. 85.

66

Other Projects

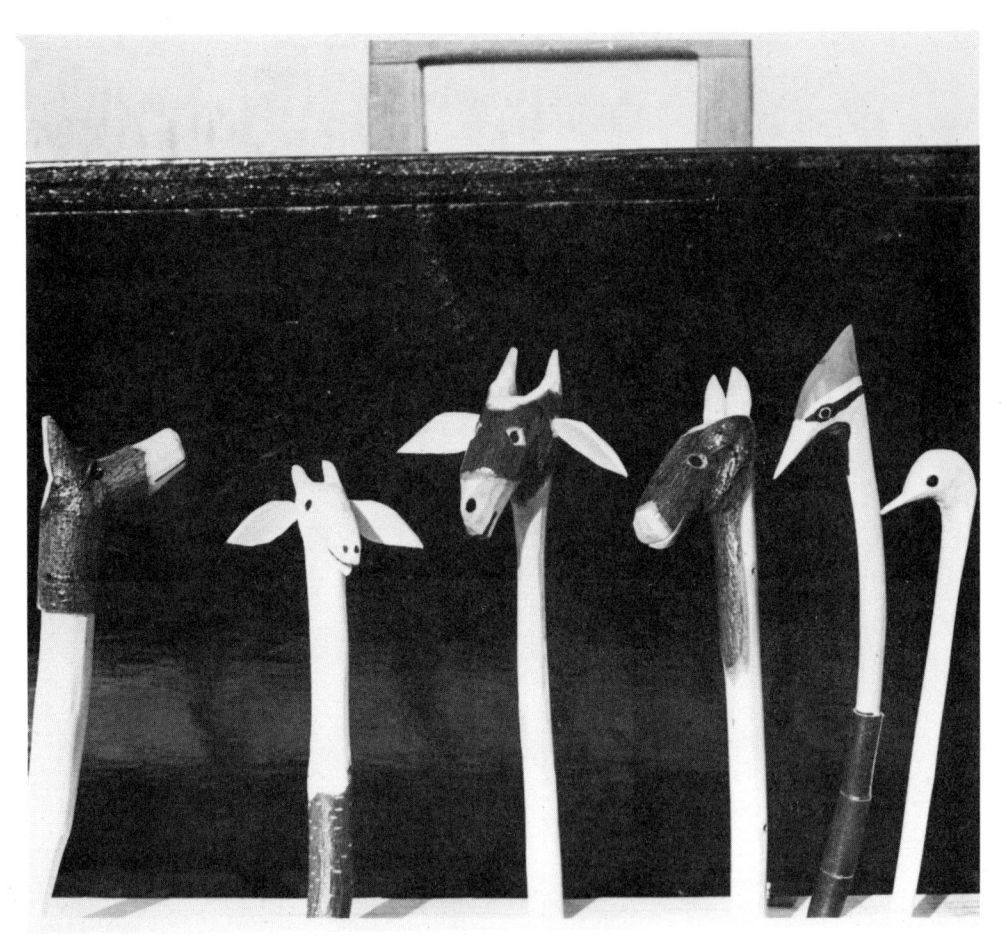

Fig. 86. Animals and birds. Remember, if you make a mistake when you're carving a rooster, you can create one of these instead.

Bow

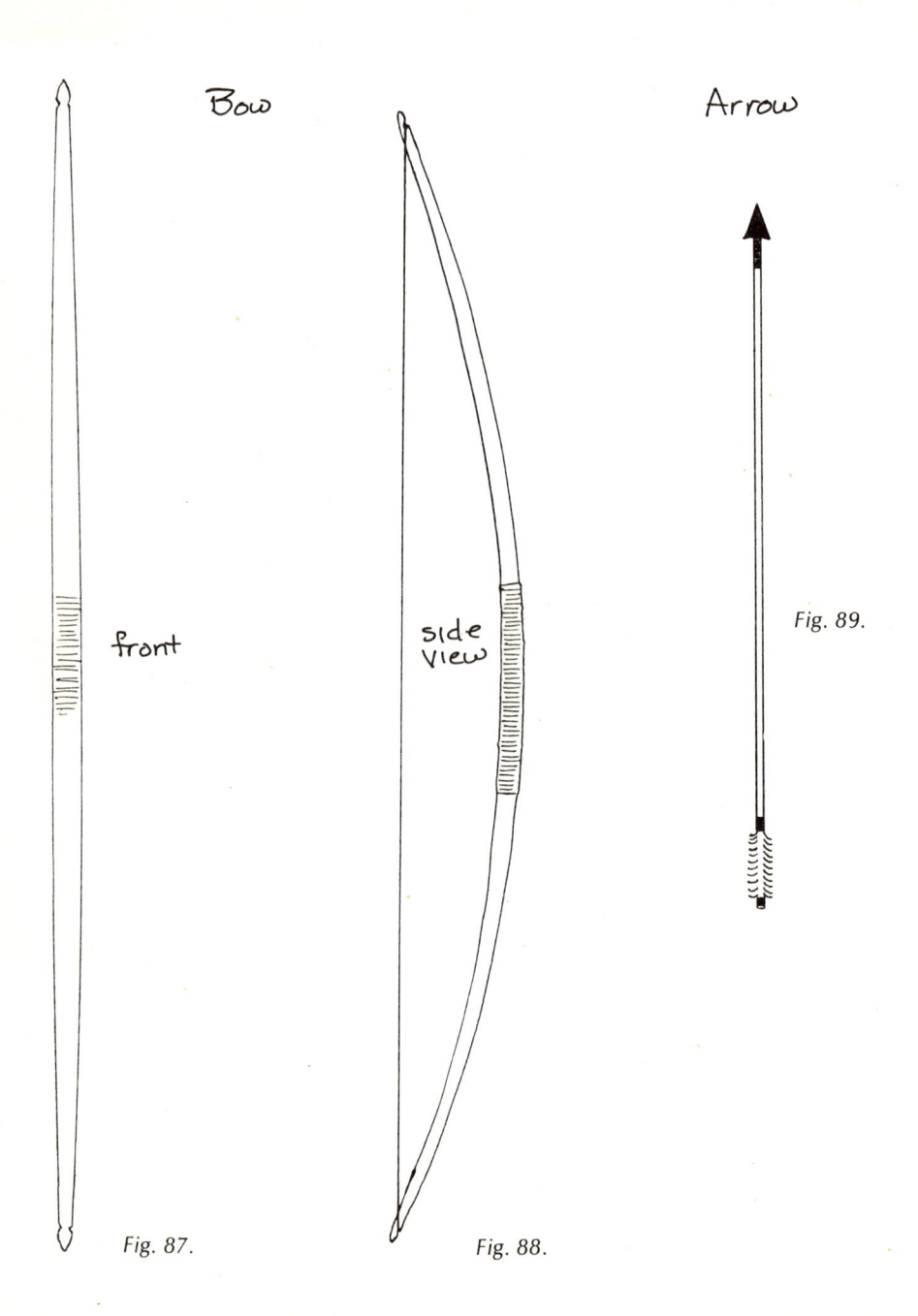

front

Fig. 87.

side view

Fig. 88.

Arrow

Fig. 89.

Other Projects

Miniature bows and arrows: For bows and arrows, you need straight twigs. A slightly bent green twig will straighten out if it is bent straight and allowed to dry in that position. For the bow, remove the bark from the twig and shape the twig. The bowstring and the hand grip in the middle of the bow are made of sewing thread. For the arrows, remove the bark from the thin, straight twigs and make small shavings on both sides of one end of the shaft for the feathers. Carve the point separately and glue it to the other end of the shaft. Paint the feathers. For more effect, glue a little bit of thread behind the arrowhead and at both ends of the feathers.

Fig. 90. You won't shoot any bears with these, but they are about the right size for many toy action figures.

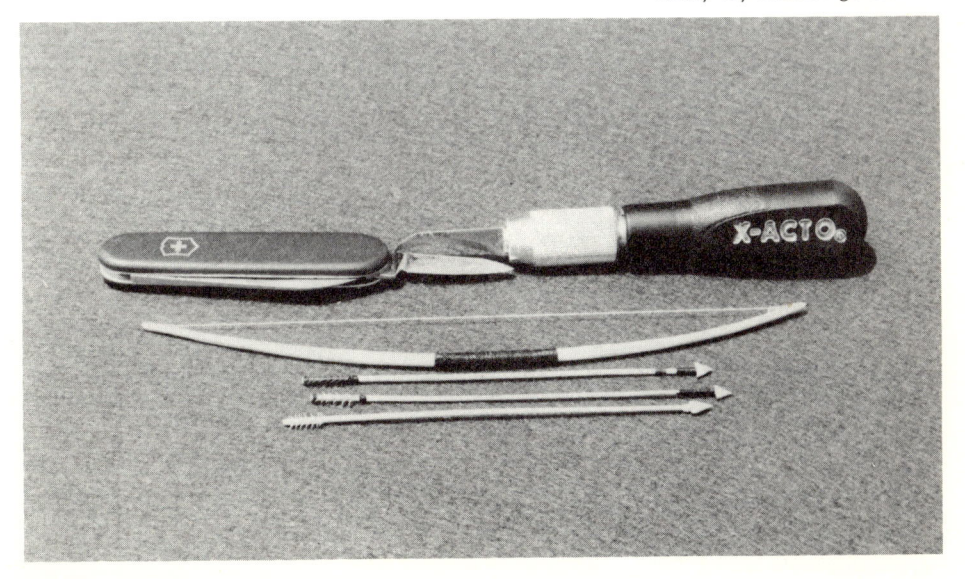

69

Carving Twigs and Branches

Fig. 91.

Lamps: It takes a bit of time to make a lamp, but it's not difficult to do. The final result is useful as well as beautiful. Be sure the branch is thoroughly dry before beginning, otherwise the finished lamp may split. Bore a hole through a 1½"–3" (38 mm–76 mm) diameter branch for the wiring. The easiest tool to use for this is an electrician's wood bit—a ¼" (6.35 mm) bit that is 18" (45.72 cm) long. If your lamp isn't too tall, you can drill both ends of the branch with regular bits so that the holes meet in the middle. Hardware and lamp fittings are readily available.

Fig. 92. These pieces of hardware and these lamp fittings are quite inexpensive and easy to find.

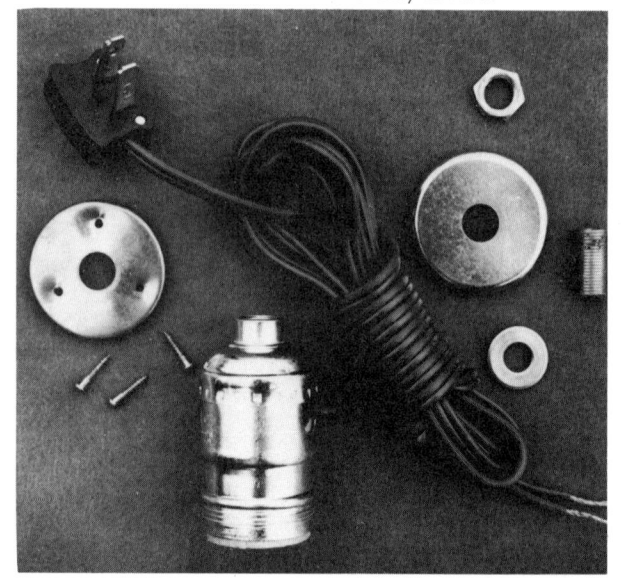

Other Projects

Unusually shaped unfinished plaques, often sold in craft and hobby shops for decoupage projects, can also be used for lamp bases. Screw the wooden base into the branch and glue it down. In order for the lamp to stand once you have wired it, glue four ¼" (6.35 mm) high wooden feet to the bottom of the base. Felt on the bottom of the feet will keep them from scratching your furniture.

You can also apply green felt to the top of the base to add a bit of color. This should be done before you attach the branch to the base. When the felt gets dirty, you can brush it clean with a toothbrush.

Fig. 93. Screw the wooden base into the branch, as well as gluing it in. Notice how the screws are countersunk. The four wooden feet enable the cord to come out under the base without danger of the lamp toppling. Felt on the bottom keeps the feet from scratching furniture.

Carving Twigs and Branches

Fig. 94. Cutting felt with a sharp knife can be easier than using scissors. Make sure you hold the felt down firmly with a straight edge.

Fig. 95. This lamp base has green felt on top.

Other Projects

Fig. 96.

73

Carving Twigs and Branches

Fig. 97. Make sure the wood you use for the salt and pepper shakers is dry.

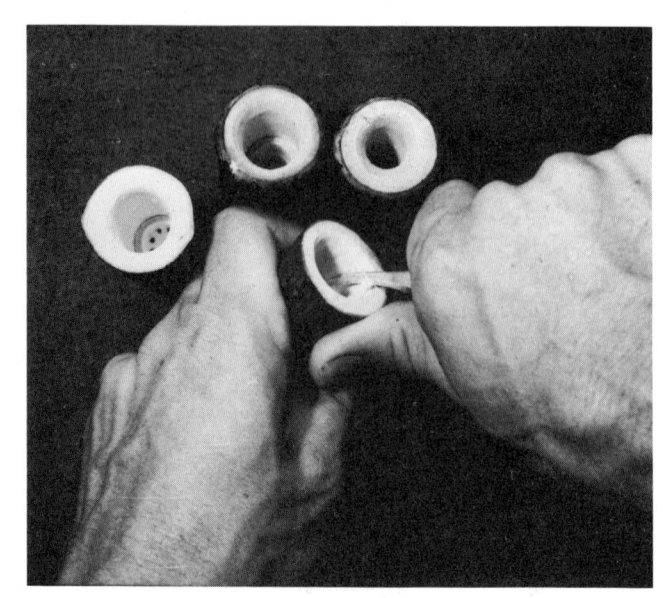

Fig. 98. Widening the holes in the shakers.

Other Projects

Salt and pepper shakers: Cut a straight, dry branch into two 2" (51 mm) or 3" (76 mm) lengths. Round the top of both pieces. Drill from the bottom with a large bit—at least ⅜" (9.53 mm) to ½" (12.70 mm)—then drill little holes in the top of the shakers. You might want to make slightly larger holes in the salt shaker. Widen the base of the large holes to be able to insert and remove the cork stoppers more easily. Corks to fit your shakers can be found in hardware stores. You may need to shorten the corks a little for the best fit. A little tray to hold the shakers adds a lot to the appeal of this particular project.

Fig. 99. Notice the distinctive touch the tray adds to this project. A rooster sitting on top of the handle lends a farmhouse touch.

75

Carving Twigs and Branches

Stockade toothpick holder: Cut straight twigs into 1½" (38 mm) or 2" (51 mm) lengths. Round one end of each. Cut a small strip of felt just a bit shorter than the length of the sticks and just wide enough to wrap around a little jar or pill bottle. Tie the felt to the bottle with a couple of strands of thread. Glue the little sticks to the felt. When the glue is dry, slip the stockade off the bottle and glue it to a suitable base.

Fig. 100. These particular twigs are birch.

Other Projects

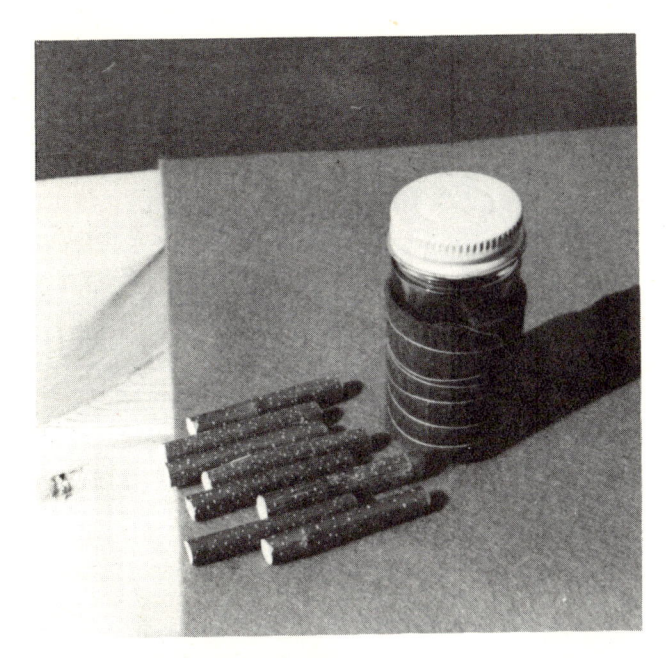

Fig. 101. Choose a color thread that won't be too obvious in any spaces between the twigs.

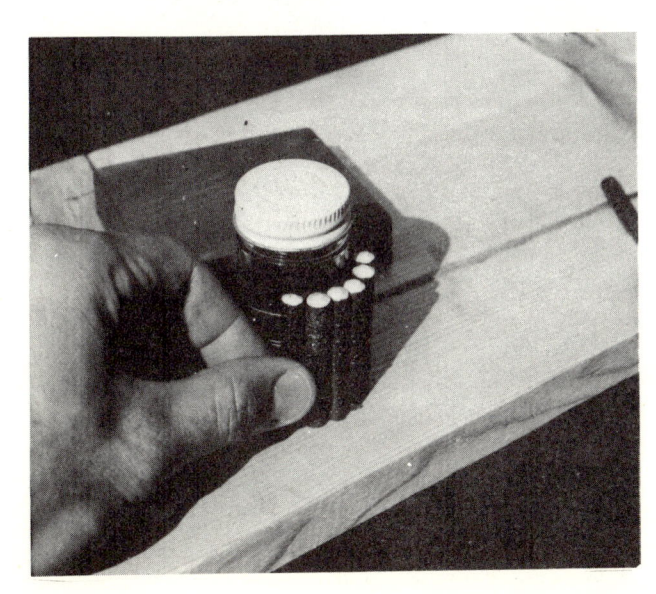

Fig. 102. Good-quality white glue or yellow carpenter's glue will hold the sticks together and will keep them attached to the felt.

77

Carving Twigs and Branches

Fig. 103. The complete stockade toothpick holder. Gluing the "stockade" to a base will further strengthen it.

Other Projects

Fig. 104. Another toothpick holder. This project takes about thirty minutes once you have a little practice making roosters and have all the pieces of wood handy.

Carving Twigs and Branches

Farmyard scene: In this scene, the plow is made by sharpening branch B and splitting branch C. A little peg is then placed between the two halves of branch C.

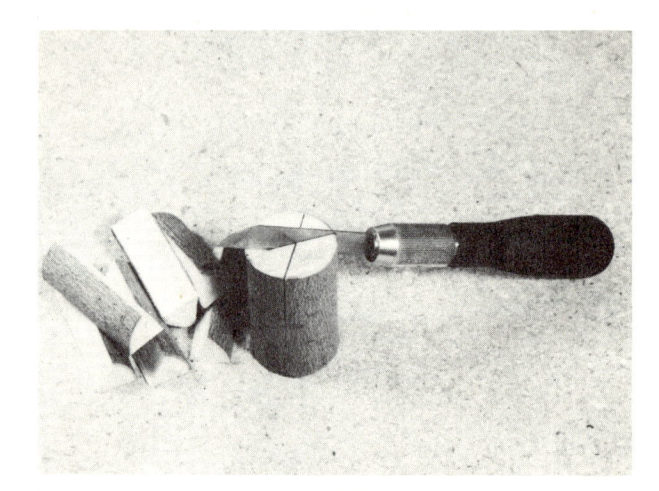

Fig. 105. Wouldn't it be great if splitting your winter wood supply were this easy?

Fig. 106. Assembling and gluing the pieces on a sheet of waxed paper will allow you to remove the whole pile of firewood and either stand it alone or glue it onto a base.

Other Projects

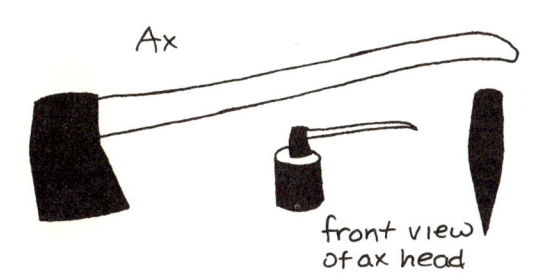

Ax

front view of ax head

Fig. 107. The ax-head and handle are two pieces of wood, carved separately and then glued together.

Fig. 108.

81

Carving Twigs and Branches

Plaques: Make the background in felt. Drill holes in the fenceposts so the rails can slip through. Another type of fence can be made by running two or three fine strands of copper wire across the plaque and gluing split halves of the fenceposts over the wire.

Fig. 109.

Other Projects

Bookends: To make bookends, begin with wood that is large enough and heavy enough to hold the weight of the books you wish to support. Bits of rubber under the bases may help bookends from slipping.

Fig. 110.

83

Carving Twigs and Branches

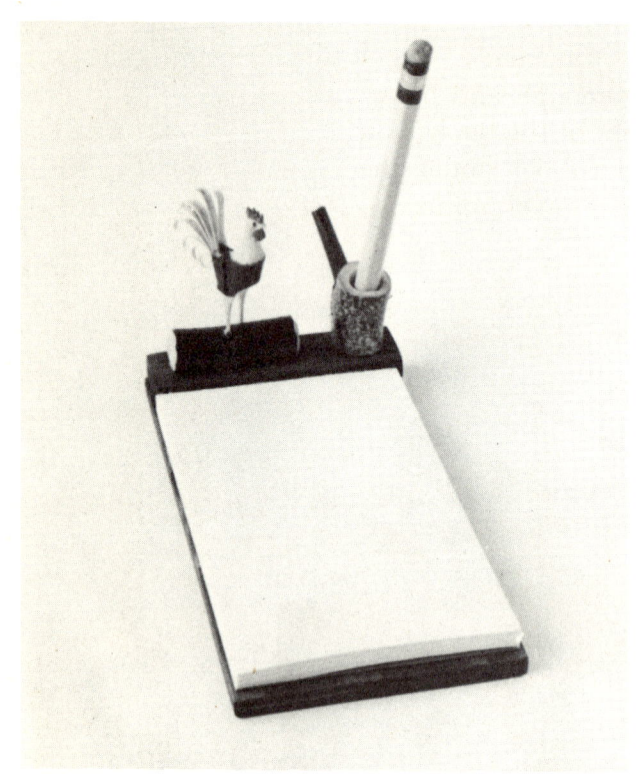

Fig. 111. In the note pad, the pad is attached to the base by two drops of glue and can be replaced easily.

Fig. 112. Penholder of logs and firewood.

Other Projects

Fig. 113. The natural groove in the scrap of millwork that serves as the base of this desk set can also hold pens and pencils.

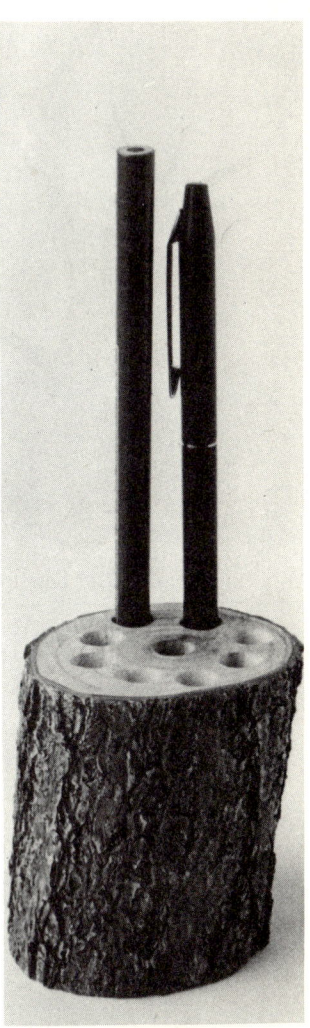

Fig. 114. Several holes drilled in a stump make a simple, but attractive, pen-and-pencil holder, especially if the stump has sharply defined growth rings. The larger the stump, the more holes you can make.

Carving Twigs and Branches

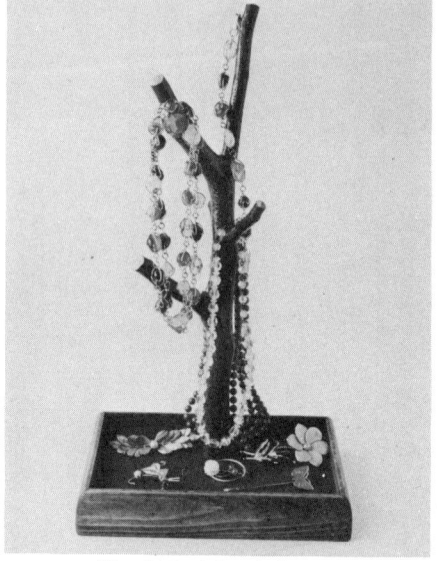

Fig. 115. A bare tree.

Fig. 116. A loaded tree.

Fig. 117. You may have to hunt a bit to find a branch suitable for making a coat rack. Just keep your eyes open.

Other Projects

Fig. 118. A twisted birch branch lent itself beautifully to this pot holder plaque.

Fig. 119. A kitchen-utensil tree.

Fig. 120. Another style jewelry tree.

87

Carving Twigs and Branches

Fig. 121.

Fig. 122. Napkin holders are very popular items, because they are practical as well as decorative.

88

Other Projects

Fig. 123.

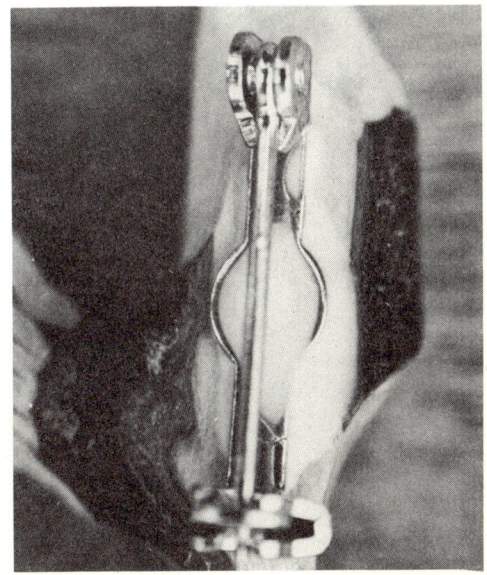

Fig. 124. To make a rooster pin or tie tack, flatten one side of the rooster (greatly enlarged here) and glue a pin back or tie tack finding to the flattened surface.

89

Carving Twigs and Branches

Letter Opener

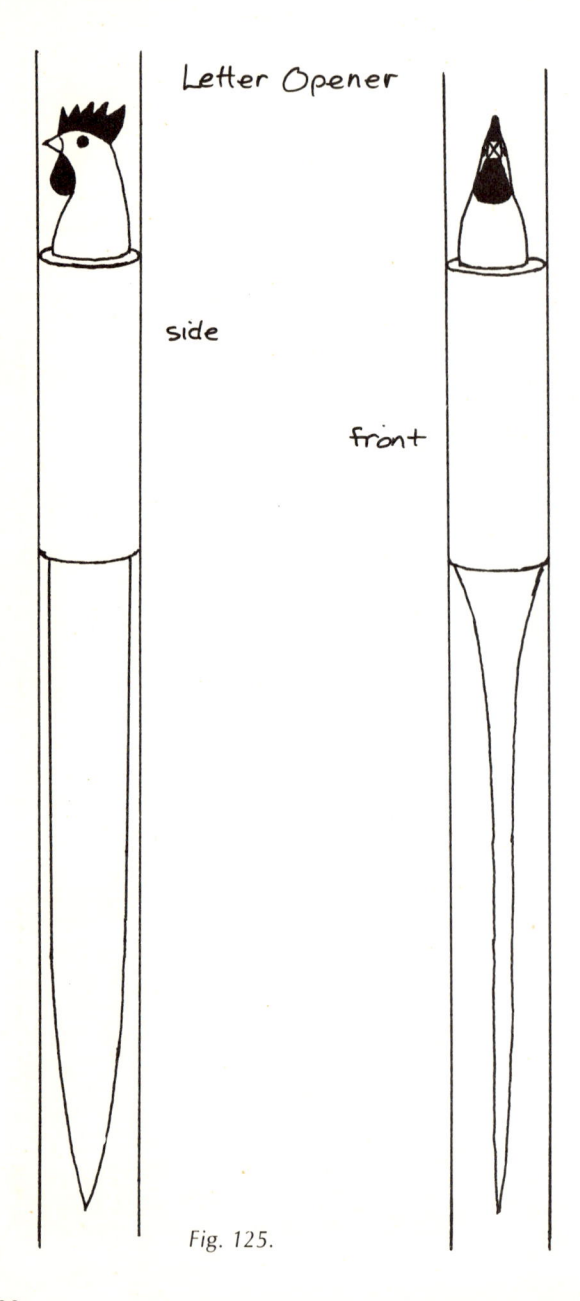

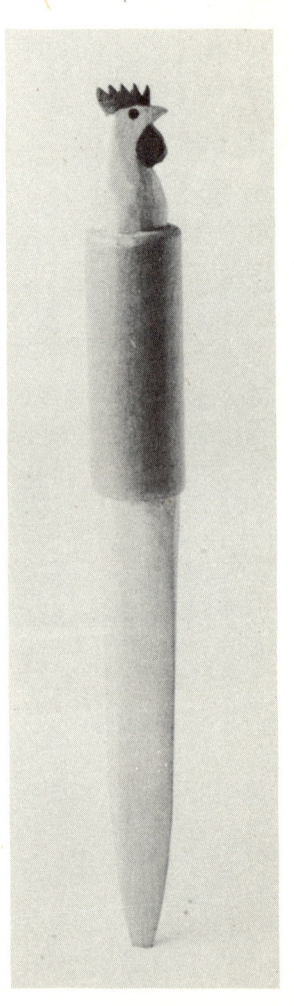

side

front

Fig. 125.

Fig. 126. A bit of sandpaper will give the blade a smooth finish.

Other Projects

Dowel projects: Some people don't have access to branches or twigs, so here are some projects that can be made from an 8" × ½" (20 cm × 12.70 mm) or 8" × ⅝" (20 cm × 15.0 mm) piece of doweling. Even an old broom handle will do.

Make a letter opener from one length of doweling. Make the pickle fork by carving from one length of doweling or by carving the fork and the rooster separately and gluing them together.

Pickle Fork

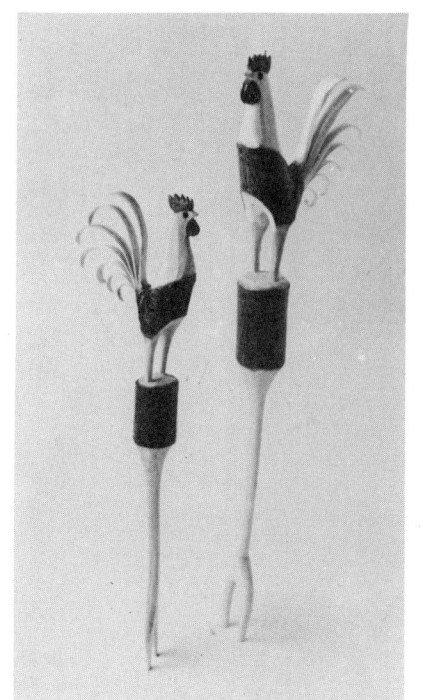

Fig. 127. Be careful carving the fork part. It can be a bit delicate.

Fig. 128.

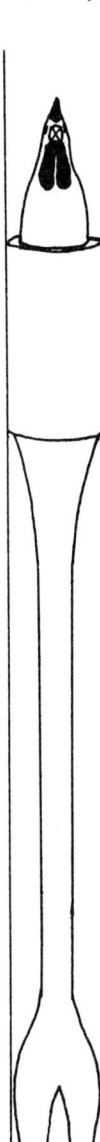

91

Carving Twigs and Branches

Fig. 129. Name-pins make simple, attractive gifts. Family nameplates can be set above doorbells, on desks, above fireplaces, and lots of other places.

Personalizing your projects: Using a woodburner, you can add a distinctive touch to many of your projects.

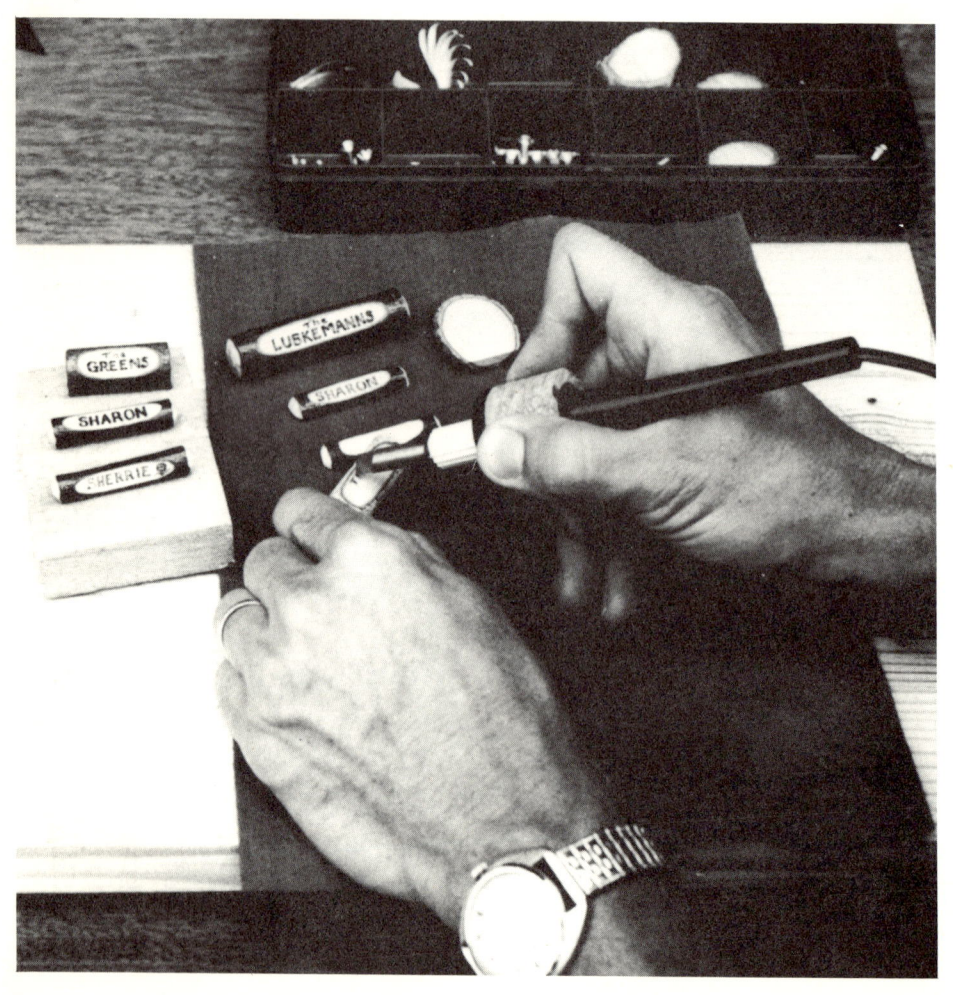

Other Projects

Fig. 130. To make this kind of eagle, you need a fairly symmetrical, three-pronged wood fork, a kind that's not always easy to find.

Carving Twigs and Branches

Fig. 131. Here's a twig man you can make.

Other Projects

Fig. 132. The author at his workbench.

INDEX

animal and bird display, 67
ax, miniature, 81
beak, 40, 41
blades, 13-14
bookends, 83
bow and arrow, mini, 68-69
branches, 10, 18-20, 26, 54
    carving, 27-47
    selecting, 17
candle holders, 51, 53
carpenter's glue, 77
carving a rooster, 27-51
chick, 56, 57
coat rack, 86
comb, 39, 40, 41
correcting mistakes, 52
crowing rooster, 41
cutting, 23-26
desk set, 85
dowel projects, 91-94
drawcutting, 24
eagle, 93
farmyard scene, 90-91
felt cutting, 72
fighting rooster, 58
giraffe, 66, 67
glue, 77
goat, 66, 67
green wood, 16
hen, 56, 57
heron, 16, 62-63
horse, 66, 67
horse penholder, 52
jewelry tree, 86, 87
kitchen-utensil tree, 29, 87
lamps, 70-73
letter opener, 65, 90, 91
log and firewood penholder, 84
logs, fallen, 52
lumberyard scraps, 55
millwork, 55, 85

name-pins, 92
napkin holders, 88
note pad, 84
pad, 84
paint, 12, 48, 49
pen, 15
pen-and-pencil holder, 85
penholder, 85
    horse, 52
    log and firewood, 84
personalizing projects, 92
pheasant, 49, 60-61
pickle fork, 91
pin, 89, 92
pith, 19
plaques, 19, 82, 89
    as lamp bases, 71
    for pot holders, 87
pocketknife, 11, 13-14
polyurethane, 51
projects, 55-94
    dowel, 90-93
rooster
    carving a, 27-55
    crowing, 41
    display of, 26
    fighting, 58
    making a stand for a, 50
    sizing and shaping a, 27
    value of, 9
rooster projects
    on bare tree, 86
    bookends, 83
    caricatures, 59
    in farmyard scene, 81
    on lamp base, 73
    pickle fork, 91
    pin, 89
    tie tack, 89
    on utensil tree, 29, 87
    with candle holder, 51, 53
    with desk set, 85
    with hen and chick, 57
    with napkin holder, 88
    with note pad, 84

    with open beak, 41
    with pot holder plaque, 87
    with salt and pepper
        shakers, 75
salt and pepper shakers, 74-75
sanding, 37
selecting wood, 17
shellac, 51
songbirds, 64
stands, 50
stockade toothpick holder, 76-78
straightaway cutting, 23
stumps, 54
    as pen- and pencil-holders,
        85
    sawed off, 51
supplies, 11-14
tail feathers, 43-47
    on fighting rooster, 58
    on pheasant, 60
thread, 77
thumbpushing, 25
tie tack, 89
toothpick holder, 76-79
tree
    bare, 86
    jewelry, 86, 87
    kitchen-utensil, 87
twig man, 94
water bird, 65
wattles, 40, 41, 42
waxed paper, 80
wood, 15-22
    types of, 18-20
wood block, 22
woodburner, 92
wood forks, 17
    three-pronged, 93
    two-pronged, 21-22
woodpecker, 65
wood selection, 17
woods, types of, 18-20
workbench, 95
X-Acto knives, 11
    for carving a rooster, 27